a little taste of...

spain

D1407084

a little taste of...

spain

Recipes by Vicky Harris

Photography by
  Martin Brigdale (location) and
  Ian Hofstetter (recipes)

Additional text by John Newton

MURDOCH BOOKS

contents

SPECIAL FEATURES

a little taste...

Let us deal first with the ridiculous notion, still occasionally voiced, that Spanish food is greasy and badly cooked. There is a simple historical explanation for this undeserved slur.

When Spain emerged in the 1950s as a destination for cheap packaged seaside holidays, English tourists quite reasonably requested their evening meal at 7 pm, a time when most respectable Spaniards are embarking on their first round of tapas: dinner, in Spain, usually begins around 10 pm. Grumpily, the locals served the tourists whatever came to hand, often indifferent chicken and chips. On such cultural misunderstandings are reputations lost.

But a case can be made for the assertion that there is no such thing as Spanish food. Spain is a political construct, made up of disparate groups with their own languages, cultures — and cuisines. Take as an example the dish that has reluctantly been cast as Spain's national food — paella. The original paella is a regional dish, found in the province of Valencia. However, as with many Spanish dishes, there are marked variations across the length and breadth of the country, with varying degrees of success. Another example can be found in Spain's north-western provinces, bordering the Atlantic, where the olive tree is unknown. As a result, most traditional dishes are lubricated with pork fat.

Still in the north but to the east, live the Basques whose obsession with food is such that, at the end of a day's toil, men will gather in gastronomy clubs to cook for each other. The Basque capital, San Sebastián, is for many the culinary capital of Spain, if not the world, and restaurants are strewn with Michelin stars (at times more per capita than Paris), while the tapas bars (known locally as *pinchos*) serve exquisite miniature creations to standing diners.

Head south through Catalonia and discover deeply traditional cuisine living in harmony with some of the most revolutionary modern food being created on the planet, at, for example, *El Bulli* restaurant in Rosas, north of Barcelona. Keep travelling south to Andalusia and you will see that the frying of seafood in olive oil has been raised to a high art and that gazpacho can also be white.

And everywhere, the cheeses — over 100 different types. Many more are made and consumed locally. Perhaps the most fascinating thing about these cheeses is that they are still made by hand, the majority from milk from the cheesemakers' own herds.

And if the cheese is a revelation, the wine is a benediction. There are currently 54 *Denominación de Origen* (DO) winemaking areas, producing a profusion of wines from traditional and new world grapes. From the cavas of Catalonia to the sherries of Jerez, there's no shortage of accompaniments to the remarkable food you will find in Spain.

a little taste of...

In even the most ordinary tapas bar (or *tasca*) in a small town or one of the outer *barrios* (suburbs) of a large town, you are able to choose from a dazzling array of tapas. Laid out along the bar behind a glass case will be piles of purple mussels, curled coils of prawns (shrimp) and shimmering stacks of sardines. Hanging overhead, succulent legs of *jamón serrano* (cured ham), strings of sausages, chillies like firecrackers, and plump red dried capsicums (peppers).

Without a word of Spanish, you can order by pointing at such dishes as *gambas al ajillo*, sizzling clay pots of prawns cooked in olive oil and immoral quantities of garlic, and *chorizo en sidra*, a speciality from the mountainous northern province of Asturias. If you have any room, a slice of tortilla, the simple and delicious omelette of potato, onion and garlic, is as Spanish, as earthy and as rich as flamenco.

...the tapas bar

gambas al ajillo

1.25 kg (2 lb 12 oz) raw prawns (shrimp)
80 g (2¾ oz) butter, melted
185 ml (6 fl oz/¾ cup) olive oil
8 garlic cloves, crushed
2 spring onions (scallions), thinly sliced
crusty bread, to serve

Serves 4

Preheat the oven to 250°C (500°F/Gas 9). Peel the prawns, leaving the tails intact. Pull out the vein from the back, starting at the head end. Cut a slit down the back of each prawn.

Combine the butter and oil and divide among four 500 ml (17 fl oz/2 cup) cast-iron pots. Divide half the crushed garlic among the pots.

Place the pots on a baking tray and heat in the oven for 10 minutes, or until the mixture is bubbling. Remove from the oven and divide the prawns and remaining garlic among the pots. Return to the oven for 5 minutes, or until the prawns are cooked. Stir in the spring onion. Season to taste. Serve with bread to mop up the juices.

3 teaspoons olive oil
1 small onion, finely chopped
1½ teaspoons sweet paprika (pimentón)
125 ml (4 fl oz/½ cup) dry alcoholic apple
  cider
60 ml (2 fl oz/¼ cup) chicken stock
1 bay leaf
280 g (10 oz) chorizo, sliced diagonally
2 teaspoons sherry vinegar, or to taste
2 teaspoons chopped flat-leaf (Italian)
  parsley

Serves 4

Heat the oil in a saucepan over low heat, add the onion and cook for 3 minutes, or until soft, stirring occasionally. Add the paprika and cook for 1 minute.

Increase the heat to medium, add the cider, stock and bay leaf to the pan and bring to the boil. Reduce the heat and simmer for 5 minutes. Add the chorizo and simmer for 5 minutes, or until the sauce has reduced slightly. Stir in the sherry vinegar and parsley. Serve hot.

chorizo en sidra

pan con tomate

1 crusty bread stick
6 garlic cloves, halved
3 tomatoes, halved
extra virgin olive oil, for drizzling

Serves 6

Slice the bread stick diagonally and toast the slices very lightly. Rub them on one side with a cut garlic clove, then with half a tomato, squeezing the juice onto the bread. Season with a little salt and drizzle with extra virgin olive oil. Serve as part of a tapas, or as a simple snack.

175 g (6 oz) minced (ground) pork
175 g (6 oz) minced (ground) veal
3 garlic cloves, crushed
35 g (1¼ oz/⅓ cup) dry breadcrumbs
1 teaspoon ground coriander
1 teaspoon ground nutmeg
1 teaspoon ground cumin
pinch of ground cinnamon
1 egg
2 tablespoons olive oil

SPICY TOMATO SAUCE
1 tablespoon olive oil
1 onion, chopped
2 garlic cloves, crushed
125 ml (4 fl oz/½ cup) dry white wine
400 g (14 oz) tin chopped tomatoes
1 tablespoon tomato paste
   (concentrated purée)
125 ml (4 fl oz/½ cup) chicken stock
½ teaspoon cayenne pepper
80 g (2¾ oz/½ cup) frozen peas

Serves 6

Combine the pork, veal, garlic, breadcrumbs, spices, egg and some salt and pepper in a bowl. Mix by hand until the mixture is smooth and leaves the side of the bowl. Refrigerate, covered, for 30 minutes.

Roll tablespoons of the mixture into balls. Heat 1 tablespoon of olive oil in a frying pan and toss half the meatballs over medium–high heat for 2–3 minutes, or until browned. Drain on paper towels. Add the remaining oil, if necessary, and brown the rest of the meatballs. Drain on paper towels.

To make the sauce, heat the oil in a frying pan over medium heat and cook the onion, stirring occasionally, for 3 minutes, or until translucent. Add the garlic and cook for 1 minute. Increase the heat to high, add the wine and boil for 1 minute. Add the crushed tomatoes, tomato paste and stock and simmer for 10 minutes. Stir in the cayenne pepper, peas and meatballs and simmer for 5–10 minutes, or until the sauce is thick. Serve hot.

albóndigas

tapas traditions... There is much more to tapas than an alluring array of tiny dishes. Tapas is a way of life as much as a way of eating, a convivial way of filling the gap between the end of work and the beginning of the evening meal; a leisurely stroll with friends, from bar to bar, sipping tiny glasses of *fino* (sherry) or beer between delicious mouthfuls.

Tapas is the fast food of the gods. Relaxed. Delicious. Unhurried. The tapas philosophy lounges comfortably in the opposite corner from the time-obsessed world of rushed frozen dinners. Paradoxically, tapas also prove that fast food can be good food.

In the beginning, tapas were free snacks handed out by the innkeepers of Andalusia with the evening glass of chilled sherry or wine. Nothing elaborate, just a slice of chorizo sausage or Manchego cheese on a hunk of coarse country bread. Stop for a glass of wine or a beer in a *bodega* (inn) or bar in Andalusia today, and chances are this is what you will be given.

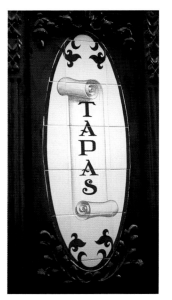

The noun tapas is from the verb *tapear* (to cover), alluding to the old Andalusian habit of covering a glass of wine or sherry with a slice of sausage or ham. Today, the habit of wandering from bar to bar is known in the south of Spain as *tapeando*, literally, 'tapasing'.

In the north of Spain, in the Basque country, tapas are known as *pinchos*, meaning skewers, for the simple reason that many northern Spanish tapas are skewered, and the tapas crawl is known as the *chiquiteo* or, in the Basque language, *txikiteo*.

But wherever you find it, the tapas bar will be packed with locals arguing about politics and football, sipping glasses of cold sherry or beer and nibbling from the contents of an array of little oval-shaped plates — known as *barcos* (boats) — spread out in front of them.

Go in for a drink or a coffee, or both, and then stay for as long as you like watching the passers-by, brushing up on your Spanish, listening to the old men in the corner passing conversation around the table carefully, as though it were a precious vessel — and in Spain, it is: Miguel de Unamuno, philosopher, poet, novelist and critic, wrote that 'Spanish culture is to be found in the cafés more often than the universities'.

salted almonds

1 egg white
¹/₄ teaspoon sweet paprika (pimentón)
500 g (1 lb 2 oz) whole blanched almonds
1¹/₂ tablespoons coarse sea salt grains
  (not flakes)

Serves 6–8

Preheat the oven to 120°C (235°F/Gas ¹/₂). In a large bowl, lightly whip the egg white and paprika with a fork until the mixture starts to froth. Add the blanched almonds and toss to coat evenly.

Divide the nuts between two non-stick baking trays. Sprinkle with the sea salt, turning the nuts several times so that the salt adheres to them. Spread over the trays. Bake for 30 minutes, turning the nuts over occasionally to prevent them from sticking. Turn off the heat and leave the almonds in the oven for 30 minutes. When completely cooled, store in airtight jars.

90 g (3¼ oz) butter
1 small onion, finely chopped
115 g (4 oz) open cap mushrooms,
   finely chopped
125 g (4½ oz/1 cup) plain (all-purpose)
   flour
250 ml (9 fl oz/1 cup) milk
185 ml (6 fl oz/¾ cup) chicken stock
115 g (4 oz) jamón or prosciutto,
   finely chopped
60 g (2¼ oz/½ cup) plain (all-purpose)
   flour, extra
2 eggs, lightly beaten
50 g (1¾ oz/½ cup) dry breadcrumbs
oil, for deep-frying

Makes 24

Melt the butter in a saucepan over low heat, add the onion and cook for 5 minutes, or until translucent. Add the mushrooms and cook over low heat, stirring occasionally, for 5 minutes. Add the flour and stir over medium–low heat for 1 minute, or until the mixture is dry and crumbly and begins to change colour. Remove from the heat and gradually add the milk, stirring until smooth. Stir in the stock and return to the heat, stirring until the mixture boils and thickens. Stir in the jamón and some black pepper, then transfer the mixture to a bowl to cool for about 2 hours.

Roll heaped tablespoons of the mixture into croquette shapes about 6 cm (2½ inches) long. Put the extra flour, beaten egg and breadcrumbs in three separate shallow bowls. Toss the croquettes in the flour, dip in the egg, allowing the excess to drain away, then roll in the breadcrumbs. Put on a baking tray and refrigerate for about 30 minutes.

Fill a deep, heavy-based saucepan one-third full of oil and heat to 170°C (325°F), or until a cube of bread dropped into the oil browns in 20 seconds. Add the croquettes in batches and deep-fry for 3 minutes, turning, until brown. Drain well on paper towel. Serve hot.

croquetas

broad beans with jamón

20 g (¾ oz) butter
1 onion, chopped
175 g (6 oz) jamón or prosciutto,
   roughly chopped
2 garlic cloves, crushed
500 g (1 lb 2 oz) broad (fava) beans,
   fresh or frozen
125 ml (4 fl oz/½ cup) dry white wine
185 ml (6 fl oz/¾ cup) chicken stock

Serves 4

Melt the butter in a large saucepan and add the onion, jamón and garlic. Cook over medium heat for 5 minutes, stirring often, until the onion softens.

Add the broad beans and wine and cook over high heat until reduced by half. Add the stock, reduce the heat, cover and cook for about 10 minutes. Uncover and simmer for another 10 minutes. Serve warm as a tapas dish with crusty bread, or hot as a side dish.

3 garlic cloves, thinly sliced
2 tablespoons vinegar or lemon juice
500 g (1 lb 2 oz) cured (wrinkled)
  black olives
1 handful chopped flat-leaf (Italian)
  parsley
1 tablespoon chilli flakes
3 teaspoons crushed coriander seeds
2 teaspoons crushed cumin seeds
500 ml (17 fl oz/2 cups) olive oil

Fills a 1 litre (35 fl oz/4 cup) jar

Soak the garlic slices in the vinegar or lemon juice for 24 hours. Drain and mix in a bowl with the olives, parsley, chilli flakes, coriander and cumin.

Sterilize a 1 litre (35 fl oz/4 cup) wide-necked jar by rinsing it with boiling water, then drying it in a warm oven. Don't dry it with a tea towel (dish towel).

Spoon the olives into the jar and pour in the olive oil. Seal and marinate in the refrigerator for 1–2 weeks before serving at room temperature. The olives will keep for a further month in the refrigerator.

chilli olives

tuna empanadas

400 g (14 oz/3¼ cups) plain (all-purpose) flour, plus extra for rolling
75 g (2¾ oz) butter, softened
2 eggs
60 ml (2 fl oz/¼ cup) white wine
1 egg, extra, lightly beaten

FILLING
1 tablespoon olive oil
1 small onion, finely diced
2 teaspoons tomato paste (concentrated purée)

125 g (4½ oz/½ cup) tin chopped tomatoes
85 g (3 oz) tin tuna, drained
1½ tablespoons chopped roasted capsicum (pepper) (page 251)
2 tablespoons chopped flat-leaf (Italian) parsley

Makes 24

Sift the flour and 1 teaspoon of salt into a large bowl. Rub the butter into the flour until the mixture resembles fine breadcrumbs. Combine the eggs and wine and add to the bowl, cutting the liquid in with a flat-bladed knife to form a dough. Turn onto a lightly floured surface and gather together into a smooth ball (do not knead or you will have tough pastry). Cover with plastic wrap and refrigerate for 30 minutes.

To make the filling, heat the olive oil in a frying pan over medium heat and cook the onion for about 5 minutes, or until translucent. Add the tomato paste and chopped tomato and cook for 10 minutes, or until pulpy. Add the tuna, roasted capsicum and parsley and season well.

Preheat the oven to 190°C (375°F/Gas 5). Dust a work surface with the extra flour. Roll out half the pastry to a thickness of 2 mm (1/16 inch). Using a 10 cm (4 inch) cutter, cut into 12 rounds. Put a heaped tablespoon of filling on each round, fold over and brush the edges with water, then pinch to seal. Continue with the remaining rounds, then repeat with the remaining dough and filling to make 24 empanadas.

Transfer to a lightly oiled baking tray and brush each empanada with beaten egg. Bake for about 30 minutes, or until golden. Serve warm or cold.

olives and olive oil... Spanish life and cuisine are lubricated by the juice from the fruit of the olive tree. Having arrived in Spain around 1000 BC with the Phoenicians, the olive tree was further cultivated by the Romans, and then the Moors (Arabs), who occupied Spain from AD 700 to AD 1492. They brought their own varieties of olives and the Spanish words for the olive (*aceituna*) and olive oil (*aciete*).

Olives grow south of a line drawn across Spain, roughly from Gerona in the east to the Portuguese border in the west. The further south you travel, the more the landscape is carpeted with row upon row of olive trees.

Spain produces between 600 000 and 900 000 tonnes of olive oil annually, out of a global total of 2.6 million tonnes per year. Much of that oil ends up, anonymously, in the blends of other countries.

It was ever thus. Archaeologists excavating Monte Testaccio on the Tiber in Rome in the 19th century found that it was not so much a hill as a pile of around 40 million broken olive oil amphoras —from Spain. The seals indicated that the pots dated from AD 140 to AD 265.

Today, there are some 17 major varieties of olives used to make oil in Spain, four of the most popular being *arbequina*, *cornicabra*, *empeltre* and *picual*. With so many different oils, today's Spanish cook is faced with a quandary: which olive oil to use for which dish? 'The essential point,' says master chef Luis Irizar of San Sebastián, 'is how to delineate the flavours of the dish rather than take away from them. We need to ask which oil goes with which ingredient and what is the oil's function in the dish?'

But the fruit of the tree is also eaten, and on every bar in Spain you will find bowls of olives, green or black, the best cured in brine for 1–6 months. Around Christmas, the cracked green olives appear, eagerly awaited by many for whom their bitter flavour is the best of all. These are the first-picked fruit of the season, cracked with a hammer, then brine cured, often with fennel stalks. And this takes us back to the ancient Phoenicians — today's Lebanese — for whom this is also a favourite way of curing olives.

2 tablespoons lemon juice
4 large globe artichokes
2 garlic cloves, crushed
1 teaspoon finely chopped oregano
1/2 teaspoon ground cumin
1/2 teaspoon ground coriander
pinch of chilli flakes
3 teaspoons sherry vinegar
60 ml (2 fl oz/1/4 cup) olive oil

Serves 4

Add the lemon juice to a large bowl of cold water. Trim the artichokes, cutting off the stalks to within 5 cm (2 inches) of the base of each artichoke and removing the tough outer leaves. Cut off the top quarter of the leaves from each. Slice each artichoke in half from top to base, or into quarters if large. Remove each small, furry choke with a teaspoon, then place each artichoke in the bowl of acidulated water to prevent it from discolouring while you prepare the rest.

Bring a large non-aluminium saucepan of water to the boil, add the artichokes and 1 teaspoon of salt and simmer for 20 minutes, or until tender. (The cooking time will depend on the artichoke size.) Test by pressing a skewer into the base. If cooked, the artichoke will be soft and give little resistance. Strain, then drain the artichokes on their cut side while cooling.

Combine the garlic, oregano, cumin, coriander and chilli flakes in a small bowl. Season with salt and pepper and blend in the vinegar. Beating constantly, slowly pour in the olive oil to form an emulsion. This step can be done in a small food processor.

Arrange the artichokes in rows on a serving platter. Pour the dressing over the top and leave to cool completely.

alcachofas en vinagreta aromática

patatas bravas

1 kg (2 lb 4 oz) all-purpose potatoes,
  such as desiree
oil, for deep-frying
500 g (1 lb 2 oz) ripe roma (plum)
  tomatoes
2 tablespoons olive oil
¼ red onion, finely chopped
2 garlic cloves, crushed

3 teaspoons sweet paprika (pimentón)
¼ teaspoon cayenne pepper
1 bay leaf
1 teaspoon sugar
1 tablespoon chopped flat-leaf (Italian)
  parsley, to garnish (optional)

Serves 6

Peel, then cut the potatoes into 2 cm (¾ inch) cubes. Rinse, then drain well and pat completely dry. Fill a deep-fryer or large heavy-based saucepan one-third full of oil and heat to 180°C (350°F), or until a cube of bread dropped into the oil browns in 15 seconds. Cook the potato in batches for 5 minutes, or until golden. Drain well on paper towels. Do not discard the oil.

Score a cross in the base of each tomato. Put in a bowl of boiling water for 10 seconds, then plunge into cold water and peel the skin away from the cross. Chop the flesh.

Heat the olive oil in a saucepan over medium heat and cook the onion for 3 minutes, or until softened. Add the garlic, paprika and cayenne pepper and cook for 1–2 minutes, or until fragrant.

Add the tomato, bay leaf, sugar and 90 ml (3 fl oz) water and cook, stirring occasionally, for 20 minutes, or until thick and pulpy. Cool slightly and remove the bay leaf. Blend in a food processor until smooth, adding a little water if necessary. Before serving, return the sauce to the saucepan and simmer over low heat for 2 minutes, or until heated through. Season well.

Reheat the oil to 180°C (350°F) and cook the potato again, in batches, for 2 minutes, or until very crisp and golden. Drain on paper towels. This second frying makes the potato extra crispy and stops the sauce soaking in immediately. Put on a platter and cover with sauce. Garnish with the parsley and serve.

165 g (5¾ oz/¾ cup) dried chickpeas
1 bay leaf
4 cloves
1 cinnamon stick
750 ml (26 fl oz/3 cups) chicken stock
2 tablespoons olive oil
1 onion, finely chopped
1 garlic clove, crushed
pinch of dried thyme
375 g (13 oz) chorizo, chopped
   (slightly larger than the chickpeas)
1 tablespoon chopped flat-leaf (Italian)
   parsley

Serves 6

Put the chickpeas in a large bowl, cover with water and soak overnight. Drain well, then combine in a large saucepan with the bay leaf, cloves, cinnamon stick and stock. Cover completely with water, bring to the boil, then reduce the heat and simmer for 1 hour, or until the chickpeas are tender. If they need more time, add a little more water. There should be just a little liquid left in the saucepan. Drain and remove the bay leaf, cloves and cinnamon stick.

Heat the oil in a large frying pan, add the onion and cook over medium heat for 3 minutes, or until translucent. Add the garlic and thyme and cook, stirring, for 1 minute. Increase the heat to medium–high, add the chorizo and cook for 3 minutes.

Add the chickpeas to the frying pan, mix well, then stir over medium heat until they are heated through. Remove from the heat and mix in the parsley. Taste before seasoning with salt and freshly ground black pepper. This dish is equally delicious served hot or at room temperature.

chickpeas with chorizo

stuffed mussels

18 black mussels
2 teaspoons olive oil
2 spring onions (scallions), finely chopped
1 garlic clove, crushed
1 tablespoon tomato paste
    (concentrated purée)
2 teaspoons lemon juice
1 large handful chopped flat-leaf (Italian)
    parsley
75 g (2¾ oz/¾ cup) dry breadcrumbs

2 eggs, beaten
oil, for deep-frying

WHITE SAUCE
20 g (¾ oz) butter
1½ tablespoons plain (all-purpose)
    flour
2 tablespoons milk

Makes 18

Scrub the mussels and remove the hairy beards. Discard any open mussels or those that don't close when tapped on the bench. Bring 250 ml (9 fl oz/ 1 cup) water to the boil in a saucepan, add the mussels, then cover and cook for 3–4 minutes, shaking the pan occasionally, until the mussels have just opened. Remove them as soon as they open or they will be tough. Strain the cooking liquid into a pitcher until you have 80 ml (2½ fl oz/⅓ cup). Discard any unopened mussels. Remove the other mussels from their shells and discard one half shell from each. Finely chop the mussel meat.

Heat the oil in a frying pan, add the spring onion and cook for 1 minute. Add the garlic and cook for 1 minute. Stir in the mussel meat, tomato paste, lemon juice, 2 tablespoons of the parsley and salt and pepper. Set aside to cool.

To make the white sauce, melt the butter in a saucepan over low heat. Stir in the flour and cook for 1 minute, or until pale and foaming. Remove from the heat and gradually whisk in the reserved mussel liquid, the milk and some pepper. Return to the heat and cook, stirring, for 1 minute, or until the sauce boils and thickens. Reduce the heat and simmer for 2 minutes. Cool.

Spoon the mussel mixture into the shells. Top each with some of the white sauce and smooth the surface, heaping the mixture.

Combine the breadcrumbs and remaining parsley. Dip the mussels in the egg, then press in the crumbs to cover the top. Fill a deep, heavy-based saucepan one-third full of oil and heat to 180°C (350°F), or until a cube of bread browns in 15 seconds. Cook the mussels in batches for 10–15 seconds, or until lightly browned. Remove with a slotted spoon and drain well. Serve hot.

6 garlic cloves
1½ tablespoons lemon juice
650 g (1 lb 7 oz) mushrooms (such as
 button, Swiss brown or pine), sliced
60 ml (2 fl oz/¼ cup) olive oil
¼ long red chilli, finely chopped
2 teaspoons chopped flat-leaf (Italian)
 parsley

Serves 4

Crush four of the garlic cloves and thinly slice the rest. Sprinkle the lemon juice over the sliced mushrooms.

Heat the oil in a large frying pan and add the crushed garlic and chopped chilli. Stir over medium–high heat for 10 seconds, then add the mushrooms. Season and cook, stirring often, for 8–10 minutes. Stir in the sliced garlic and parsley and cook for another minute. Serve hot.

champiñones al ajillo

tortillitas de camerones

60 g (2¼ oz/½ cup) plain (all-purpose)
  flour, sifted
55 g (2 oz/½ cup) besan (chickpea flour),
  sifted
1 teaspoon sweet paprika (pimentón)
4 large eggs, lightly beaten
4 spring onions (scallions), finely chopped
1 large handful flat-leaf (Italian) parsley,
  finely chopped
500 g (1 lb 2 oz) peeled and finely
  chopped raw prawns (shrimp)
  (about 800 g (1 lb 12 oz) unpeeled)
125 ml (4 fl oz/½ cup) vegetable oil
lemon wedges, to serve

Makes 20 fritters

Combine the flours in a bowl with the paprika and make a well in the centre. Pour in the beaten egg and mix in gradually, then stir in 60 ml (2 fl oz/¼ cup) water to make a smooth batter. Add the spring onion, parsley and prawns and season well. Rest for at least 30 minutes.

Heat the oil in a deep-sided frying pan over medium–low heat. Working in batches, spoon in 2 tablespoons of batter per fritter and flatten into a thin pancake. Cook for 2–3 minutes each side, or until golden and cooked through. Remove from the pan and drain on paper towels. Repeat with the remaining batter to make 20 fritters. Season well and serve with lemon wedges.

6 mini crispy bread rolls
90 g (3¼ oz / ⅓ cup) allioli (page 250)
12 slices jamón or prosciutto
300 g (10½ oz) pimiento, cut into strips
150 g (5½ oz) Manchego cheese, thinly
   sliced

Makes 6

Cut open the bread rolls with a bread knife, leaving them hinged, then spread with the allioli.

Put two slices of jamón or prosciutto on top of the allioli, followed by some strips of pimiento and slices of Manchego. Serve immediately.

bocadillas

jerez... We should make one thing perfectly clear right from the start. Sherry, the anglicization of *jerez* (pronounced he-reth) is produced only in Spain, and only in what is known as the 'Sherry Triangle'—a very small segment of southern Andalusia bounded by the towns of Jerez de la Frontera, Puerto de Santa María and Sanlúcar de Barrameda, the last two on the Atlantic coast. Anything called 'sherry' which is not produced in this region is not sherry at all, and may be a pleasant imitation.

The production of sherry is a complex process, involving the ageing of what starts out as a fairly ordinary dry white wine using the *solera* system. A series of wines in casks, graded by age, are blended from small amounts of the oldest to larger amounts of the youngest.

If the sherry is to be a *fino*, its production also includes time spent under *flor* (flower), a growth of yeasts on the surface of the wine in the cask. Finally, all sherry is fortified with brandy.

The variety and complexity of flavours of the various styles of sherry, from the steely dry *fino* (always served chilled) or an aged and nutty *oloroso* to the lip-smacking richness of the single grape variety *Pedro Ximenez* (at its best with chocolate), are a revelation to those used only to the warm, sickly 'cream sherry' served by maiden aunts.

When to drink sherry? Well, in Andalusia, *fino* is treated as a white wine and is drunk throughout the meal—with trout or chicken, for example. *Fino* with oysters is another match made in heaven. But more often, it is drunk as an aperitif, simply with olives and cheese, or with tapas. The same goes for the other dry sherry, *manzanilla*. Like *fino*, it should also be served chilled—and fresh: these styles do not age well.

A dry *amontillado* or *palo cortado* is often served with soup, but the bigger, sweeter and heavier styles are best left to the end of the meal—the oldest and 'brownest' of *olorosos* or *amontillados* with dessert or cheese, and *Pedro Ximenez* with the richest of sweet dishes.

If you become a true aficionado, you will want to experiment with different sherries with every course, as is done in many modern restaurants in Andalusia.

Sherry is also used extensively in cooking, most notably in *riñones en Jerez*, kidneys in sherry sauce. In Andalusia, a splash of *fino* is often added to gazpacho.

calamares fritos

500 g (1 lb 2 oz) cleaned calamari tubes
185 g (6½ oz/1½ cups) plain
** (all-purpose) flour**
2 teaspoons sweet paprika (pimentón)
oil, for deep-frying
lemon wedges, to serve
allioli (page 250), to serve (optional)

Serves 4

Wash the calamari and cut into rings about 1 cm (½ inch) thick. Combine the flour and paprika. Season the calamari rings well with salt and pepper and toss in the flour to lightly coat.

Fill a deep, heavy-based saucepan one-third full of oil and heat to 180°C (350°F), or until a cube of bread dropped into the oil browns in 15 seconds. Add the calamari in batches and cook for 2 minutes, or until golden. Drain and serve hot with the lemon wedges and allioli if desired.

MAYONNAISE
2 egg yolks
1 teaspoon dijon mustard
125 ml (4 fl oz/½ cup) extra virgin
olive oil
2 tablespoons lemon juice
2 small garlic cloves, crushed

3 tinned artichoke hearts
3 all-purpose potatoes, such as desiree,
unpeeled
100 g (3½ oz) baby green beans, trimmed
and cut into 1 cm (½ inch) lengths

1 large carrot, cut into 1 cm (½ inch) dice
125 g (4½ oz) fresh peas
30 g (1 oz) cornichons, chopped
2 tablespoons baby capers, rinsed and
drained
4 anchovy fillets, finely chopped
10 black olives, each cut into 3 slices
5 whole black olives, extra, to garnish

Serves 4–6

To make the mayonnaise, use electric beaters to beat the egg yolks with the mustard and ¼ teaspoon salt until creamy. Gradually add the oil in a fine stream, beating constantly until all the oil has been added. Add the lemon juice, garlic and 1 teaspoon boiling water and beat for 1 minute, or until well combined. Season to taste.

Cut each artichoke into quarters. Rinse the potatoes, cover with salted cold water and bring to a gentle simmer. Cook for 15–20 minutes, or until tender when pierced with a knife. Drain and allow to cool slightly. Peel and set aside. When the potatoes are completely cool, cut into 1 cm (½ inch) dice.

Blanch the beans in salted boiling water until tender but still firm to the bite. Refresh in cold water, then drain thoroughly. Repeat with the carrot and peas.

Set aside a small quantity of each vegetable, including the cornichons, for the garnish and season to taste. Put the remainder in a bowl with the capers, anchovies and sliced olives. Add the mayonnaise, toss to combine and season. Arrange on a serving dish and garnish with the reserved vegetables and the whole olives.

russian salad

marinated capsicums

3 red capsicums (peppers)
3 thyme sprigs
1 garlic clove, thinly sliced
2 teaspoons roughly chopped flat-leaf
   (Italian) parsley
1 bay leaf
1 spring onion (scallion), sliced
1 teaspoon sweet paprika (pimentón)
60 ml (2 fl oz/¼ cup) extra virgin
   olive oil
2 tablespoons red wine vinegar

Serves 6

Preheat the grill (broiler). Cut the capsicums into quarters, remove the seeds and membrane and grill (broil), skin side up, until the skin blackens and blisters. Cool in a plastic bag, then peel. Slice thinly, then place in a bowl with the thyme, garlic, parsley, bay leaf and spring onion. Mix well.

Whisk together the paprika, oil, vinegar and some salt and pepper. Pour over the capsicum mixture and toss to combine. Cover and refrigerate for at least 3 hours, or preferably overnight. Remove from the refrigerator about 30 minutes before serving.

500 g (1 lb 2 oz) all-purpose potatoes,
peeled and cut into 1 cm (½ inch) slices
60 ml (2 fl oz/¼ cup) olive oil
1 onion, thinly sliced
4 garlic cloves, thinly sliced
2 tablespoons finely chopped flat-leaf
(Italian) parsley
6 eggs

Serves 6–8

Put the potato slices in a large saucepan, cover with cold water and bring to the boil over high heat. Boil for 5 minutes, then drain and set aside.

Heat the oil in a deep-sided non-stick frying pan over medium heat. Add the onion and garlic and cook for 5 minutes, or until the onion softens.

Add the potato and parsley to the pan and stir to combine. Cook over medium heat for 5 minutes, gently pressing down into the pan.

Whisk the eggs with 1 teaspoon each of salt and freshly ground black pepper and pour evenly over the potato. Cover and cook over low–medium heat for 20 minutes, or until the eggs are just set. Slide onto a serving plate or serve directly from the pan.

tortilla

banderilla

250 g (9 oz) raw tuna
1 lemon
1 tablespoon lemon juice
1 tablespoon olive oil
16 caperberries
8 green olives, stuffed with anchovies

Makes 8

Soak eight wooden skewers in cold water for 1 hour to prevent them burning during cooking. Cut the raw tuna into 24 even-sized cubes. Remove the zest from the lemon, avoiding the bitter white pith, and cut the zest into thin strips.

Combine the tuna, lemon zest, lemon juice and olive oil in a bowl.

Thread three pieces of tuna, two caperberries and one green olive onto each skewer, alternating each ingredient. Put in a non-metallic dish and pour the marinade over them. Cook under a hot grill (broiler), turning to cook each side, for 4 minutes, or until done to your liking.

500 g (1 lb 2 oz) bacalao (salt cod)
1 large all-purpose potato (200 g/7 oz),
   unpeeled
2 tablespoons milk
60 ml (2 fl oz/¼ cup) olive oil
1 small onion, finely chopped
2 garlic cloves, crushed
30 g (1 oz/¼ cup) self-raising flour
2 eggs, separated
1 tablespoon chopped flat-leaf (Italian)
   parsley
olive oil, extra, for deep-frying

Makes about 35

Soak the bacalao in plenty of cold water for about 20 hours, changing the water four or five times to remove excess saltiness.

Cook the potato in a saucepan of boiling water for 20 minutes, or until soft. When cool, peel and mash with the milk and 2 tablespoons of the olive oil.

Drain the bacalao, cut into large pieces and put in a saucepan. Cover with water, bring to the boil over high heat, then reduce the heat to medium and cook for 10 minutes, or until the fish is soft and there is a froth on the surface. Drain. When cool enough to handle, remove the skin and any bones, then mash the flesh well with a fork until flaky.

Heat the remaining oil in a small frying pan and cook the onion over medium heat for 5 minutes, or until softened and starting to brown. Add the garlic and cook for 1 minute. Remove from the heat.

Combine the potato, bacalao, onion, flour, egg yolks and parsley in a bowl and season. Whisk the egg whites until stiff, then fold into the mixture. Fill a deep-fryer or large heavy-based saucepan one-third full of olive oil and heat to 190°C (375°F), or until a cube of bread dropped into the oil browns in 10 seconds. Drop heaped tablespoons of the mixture into the oil and cook, turning once, for 2–3 minutes, or until puffed and golden. Drain well and serve immediately.

buñuelos de bacalao

patatas allioli

750 g (1 lb 10 oz) all-purpose potatoes,
  peeled
60 ml (2 fl oz/¼ cup) olive oil

ALLIOLI
2 egg yolks
2 garlic cloves, crushed
60 ml (2 fl oz/¼ cup) white wine vinegar
  or lemon juice
125 ml (4 fl oz/½ cup) vegetable oil
125 ml (4 fl oz/½ cup) olive oil

Serves 4

Preheat the oven to 200°C (400°F/Gas 6). Cut the potatoes into 4 cm
(1½ inch) cubes and put on a baking tray with the olive oil. Mix to coat
and season well. Cook in the oven for 45 minutes, or until golden. Shake
the baking tray occasionally so the potatoes bake evenly on all sides.

To make the allioli, put the egg yolks and garlic in a food processor with
1 tablespoon of the vinegar or lemon juice. While the motor is running, add
the oils in a very slow stream until you have a thick mayonnaise. If at some
point the mayonnaise becomes too thick, add the remaining vinegar or lemon
juice and continue adding the rest of the oil. Season well.

Season the potatoes and serve with the allioli dolloped over the top or
served on the side for dipping. Any leftover allioli can be kept in an airtight
container in the refrigerator for 4–5 days.

1 kg (2 lb 4 oz) boneless, skinless chicken
   thighs
1 tablespoon sweet paprika (pimentón)
2 tablespoons olive oil
8 garlic cloves, unpeeled
60 ml (2 fl oz/¼ cup) dry sherry
125 ml (4 fl oz/½ cup) chicken stock
1 bay leaf
2 tablespoons chopped flat-leaf (Italian)
   parsley

Serves 6

Trim any excess fat from the chicken and cut the thighs into thirds. Combine the paprika with some salt and pepper in a bowl, add the chicken and toss to coat.

Heat half the oil in a large frying pan over high heat and cook the garlic cloves for 1–2 minutes, or until brown. Remove from the pan. Cook the chicken in batches for 5 minutes, or until brown all over. Return all the chicken to the pan, add the sherry, boil for 30 seconds, then add the stock and bay leaf. Reduce the heat and simmer, covered, over low heat for 10 minutes.

Meanwhile, squeeze the garlic pulp into a mortar and pestle or small bowl. Add the parsley and pound or mix with a fork to form a paste. Stir into the chicken, then cover and cook for 10 minutes, or until tender. Serve hot.

chicken in garlic sauce

scrambled eggs
with asparagus

2 garlic cloves, chopped
1 thick slice bread, crusts removed
60 ml (2 fl oz/¼ cup) olive oil
175 g (6 oz/1 bunch) asparagus, cut into
 2 cm (¾ inch) lengths
1 teaspoon sweet paprika (pimentón)
2 tablespoons white wine vinegar
6 eggs

Serves 4

Put the garlic and bread in a food processor or mortar and pestle and grind to a loose paste, adding a small amount of water (1–2 tablespoons).

Heat the oil in a frying pan and sauté the asparagus over medium heat for 2 minutes, or until just starting to become tender. Add the garlic paste, paprika, vinegar and a pinch of salt, and stir to combine. Cover and cook over medium heat for 2–3 minutes, or until the asparagus is tender.

Beat the eggs and add to the pan. Reduce the heat to low and leave to set for 1 minute, then gently fold the cooked egg over the raw egg. Repeat this several times over 4–5 minutes. Season to taste and serve immediately.

a little taste of...

Spain's 8000 kilometres (4968 miles) of coastline stretches from France to Africa, and is lapped by the Mediterranean, the Atlantic Ocean and the Cantabrian Sea. This geography and a history of invasions and occupations by Phoenicians, Greeks, Romans, Moors, Jews and finally, that diverse and pestilential clan—tourists—explains the variety of dishes and cuisines to be found along the Spanish coast and on the Balearic Islands. The elaborate Catalan seafood stew *zarzuela*, named after a Spanish form of light opera, appears as a simplified tuna-based dish (*marmitako*) in the kitchens of the Basque regions. A dish of octopus in almond sauce reminds us of medieval Moorish dishes, which mixed the sweet and the savoury. The Andalusian dish of fish baked in salt (*doradas a la sal*) derives, apparently, from the ancient Greek custom of covering fish with mud to protect them from the heat of a wood-fired oven.

...cocina de la costa

zarzuela

300 g (10½ oz) red mullet fillets
400 g (14 oz) firm white fish fillets
300 g (10½ oz) cleaned squid tubes
1.5 litres (52 fl oz/6 cups) fish stock
80 ml (2½ fl oz/⅓ cup) olive oil
1 onion, chopped
6 garlic cloves, chopped
1 small red chilli, chopped
1 teaspoon sweet paprika (pimentón)
pinch of saffron threads
150 ml (5 fl oz) white wine
400 g (14 oz) tin chopped tomatoes
16 raw prawns (shrimp), peeled and
   deveined, tails intact
2 tablespoons brandy

24 black mussels, cleaned
1 tablespoon chopped flat-leaf (Italian)
   parsley, to garnish

PICADA
2 tablespoons olive oil
2 slices day-old bread, cubed
2 garlic cloves
5 whole blanched almonds, toasted
2 tablespoons flat-leaf (Italian) parsley

Serves 6–8

Cut the fish and calamari into 4 cm (1½ inch) pieces. Pour the stock into a large saucepan, bring to the boil and boil for 15–20 minutes, or until reduced by half.

To make the picada, heat the olive oil in a frying pan, add the bread and stir for 2–3 minutes, or until golden, adding the garlic for the last minute. Process the bread, garlic, almonds and parsley in a food processor and add enough of the stock to make a smooth paste.

Heat 2 tablespoons of the oil in a large saucepan, add the onion, garlic, chilli and paprika, and cook, stirring, for 1 minute. Add the saffron, white wine, tomato and remaining stock. Bring to the boil, then reduce the heat and leave to simmer.

Heat the remaining oil in another frying pan over medium heat and cook the fish and calamari for 3–5 minutes. Remove. Add the prawns, cook for 1 minute, then pour in the brandy. Carefully ignite the brandy and let the flames burn down. Remove the seafood from the pan.

Add the mussels to the hot stock and simmer, covered, for 2–3 minutes, or until opened. Discard any that do not open. Return all the seafood to the pan, add the picada, and stir until the sauce has thickened slightly and the seafood is cooked. Season to taste. Serve garnished with parsley.

400 g (14 oz) bacalao (salt cod)
1 red capsicum (pepper)
1 tablespoon olive oil
1 small onion, chopped
1 garlic clove, crushed
¼ teaspoon dried chilli flakes
1 teaspoon sweet paprika (pimentón)
60 ml (2 fl oz/¼ cup) dry white wine
2 ripe tomatoes, finely chopped
1 tablespoon tomato paste
   (concentrated purée)
1 tablespoon chopped flat-leaf (Italian)
   parsley

Serves 6

Soak the bacalao in plenty of cold water for about 20 hours, changing the water four or five times to remove excess saltiness.

Add the cod to a saucepan of boiling water and boil for 5 minutes. Drain and leave for 10 minutes, or until cool enough to handle. Remove the skin and flake the fish into large pieces, removing any bones. Transfer to a bowl.

Preheat the grill (broiler). Cut the capsicum into quarters, remove the seeds and membrane and grill (broil), skin side up, until the skin blackens and blisters. Put in a plastic bag and leave to cool, then peel away the skin. Slice thinly.

Heat the oil in a saucepan over medium heat, add the onion and cook, stirring occasionally, for 3 minutes, or until translucent. Add the garlic, chilli flakes and paprika and cook for 1 minute. Increase the heat to high, add the white wine and simmer for 30 seconds. Reduce the heat, add the tomato and tomato paste and cook, stirring occasionally, for 5 minutes, or until thick.

Add the bacalao, cover and simmer for about 5 minutes. Gently stir in the sliced capsicum and parsley and taste before seasoning with salt. Serve hot.

bacalao with red capsicum

fish baked in salt

1.8 kg (4 lb) whole fish (such as blue-eye,
   jewfish, sea bass, groper), scaled and
   cleaned
2 lemons, sliced
4 thyme sprigs
1 fennel bulb, thinly sliced
3 kg (6 lb 12 oz) rock salt
allioli (page 250), to serve (optional)

Serves 4–6

Preheat the oven to 200°C (400°F/Gas 6). Rinse the fish and pat dry inside and out with paper towels. Put the lemon, thyme and fennel inside the cavity.

Pack half the salt into a large baking dish and put the fish on top. Cover with the remaining salt, pressing down until the salt is packed firmly around the fish.

Bake the fish for 30–40 minutes, or until a skewer inserted into the centre of the fish comes out hot. Carefully remove the salt from the top of the fish and move to one side of the dish. Peel the skin away, ensuring that no salt remains on the flesh. Serve hot or cold with allioli or your choice of accompaniment.

1 ripe tomato
125 ml (4 fl oz/½ cup) white wine
1 red onion, chopped
12–16 black mussels, bearded and
    scrubbed
125 ml (4 fl oz/½ cup) olive oil
½ red onion, extra, finely chopped
1 slice bacon, finely chopped
4 garlic cloves, crushed
1 red capsicum (pepper), finely chopped
90 g (3¼ oz) chorizo, thinly sliced
pinch of cayenne pepper
220 g (7¾ oz/1 cup) paella or medium-
    grain rice

¼ teaspoon saffron threads
500 ml (17 fl oz/2 cups) chicken stock,
    heated
85 g (3 oz) fresh or frozen peas
12 raw prawns (shrimp), peeled and
    deveined
2 squid tubes, cleaned and cut into rings
115 g (4 oz) skinless firm white fish
    fillets, cut into pieces
2 tablespoons finely chopped flat-leaf
    (Italian) parsley

Serves 4

Score a cross in the base of the tomato. Place in a bowl of boiling water for 10 seconds, then plunge into cold water and peel away the skin from the cross. Chop the tomato and set aside.

Heat the wine and onion in a saucepan. Add the mussels, cover and gently shake the pan for 5 minutes over high heat. Remove from the heat, discard any closed mussels and drain, reserving the liquid.

Heat the oil in a large heavy-based frying pan, add the extra onion, bacon, garlic and capsicum, and cook for about 5 minutes. Add the chopped tomato, chorizo and cayenne pepper. Season. Stir in the reserved liquid, then add the rice and stir again.

Blend the saffron with the stock, then stir into the rice mixture. Bring to the boil, then reduce the heat to low and simmer, uncovered, for 15 minutes without stirring.

Put the peas, prawns, squid and fish on top of the rice. Push them in, cover and cook over low heat for 10 minutes, turning over halfway through, until the rice is tender and the seafood is cooked through. Add the mussels for the last 5 minutes to heat through. If the rice is not quite cooked, add extra stock and cook for a few more minutes. Leave to rest for 5 minutes, then add the parsley and serve.

seafood paella

sardinas murcianas

1 kg (2 lb 4 oz) ripe tomatoes
24 fresh large sardines, cleaned, with
    backbones, heads and tails removed
2 green capsicums (peppers), cored,
    seeded and cut into thin rings
1 onion, sliced into thin rings
2 all-purpose potatoes, cut into 5 mm
    (¼ inch) slices
2 tablespoons chopped flat-leaf (Italian)
    parsley

3 garlic cloves, crushed
¼ teaspoon saffron threads, lightly
    toasted
2 tablespoons olive oil
chopped flat-leaf (Italian) parsley,
    extra, to garnish

Serves 6

Score a cross in the base of each tomato. Put in a bowl of boiling water for
10 seconds, then plunge into cold water and peel away the skin from the
cross. Cut each tomato into thin slices.

Preheat the oven to 180°C (350°F/Gas 4). Lightly oil a large, shallow
earthenware or ceramic baking dish wide enough to hold the length of the
sardines. Open out the sardines and lightly sprinkle the insides with salt.
Fold them back into their original shape.

Cover the base of the baking dish with a third of the tomatoes. Layer half the
sardines on top. Follow with a layer of half the capsicum, then half the onion,
then half the potatoes. Sprinkle with half the parsley and garlic, and season
with freshly ground black pepper. Crumble half the saffron over the top.

Layer the remaining sardines, half the remaining tomatoes and then the other
ingredients as before. Finish with the last of the tomatoes. Season well with
salt and freshly ground black pepper. Drizzle the oil over the surface and
cover with foil. Bake for 1 hour, or until the potatoes are cooked. Spoon off
any excess liquid, sprinkle with parsley and serve straight from the dish.

bacalao... 1000 years ago, Basque fishermen regularly set off from the coast of northern Spain to Newfoundland, off the eastern coast of Canada, a distance of some 4500 kilometres (2795 miles). Their original quarry was whales, whale meat being a delicacy in medieval times. But soon they became aware of a fishery so vast that it was said you could step off a boat and walk across the water on the backs of the fish swarming in the icy waters. The fish were Atlantic cod.

The cod were transported to the markets of Europe using the same methods as for whale meat—salting and drying the fish where it was caught. The result, bacalao, became a staple of the Spanish and Portuguese table for Lent, and an answer to devout Catholic prayers for an economical fish for the Friday abstention meal.

In 1992, after a millennium of exploitation, the vast fisheries off Newfoundland collapsed, and have yet to recover. Bacalao, now from Norway, is no longer a cheap staple, but a luxury for connoisseurs.

Why eat bacalao when fresh fish is so available? Why eat ham when you can eat pork? It is a separate product, much loved for its unique flavour and texture, and for the dishes that have evolved around it.

Cooking bacalao is not a straightforward process. First, you must choose a well-cured piece —and beware of the cheaper but inferior product made from ling fish. Well-cured bacalao is best bought from Portuguese or Spanish sources. It has white, flexible meat, dark skin and a unique smell; the best cuts tend to appear around Easter. But before you cook your bacalao, you must prepare it.

There are two ways to do this. One is to cook it over coals until it goes soft and damp. It is then easy to remove the bones and skin, and to rinse the flesh in water to remove excess salt.

The second way, the time-honoured method, is to submerge the fish in fresh water for about 20 hours, changing the water four or five times, then to poach it in water no hotter than 65°C (150°F) for 45 minutes. This is also a good test of the quality of your bacalao. If it is poor quality, it will collapse into a fibrous mass in the water. You must then take it back to the person who sold it to you and throw it at them. If it is good quality, it will emerge smooth, firm and white — and without the over-salted flavour of many badly cooked bacalao dishes.

There are almost as many Basque recipes for bacalao as there were cod fish in the North Atlantic. The most famous is bacalao *pil pil* which is, quite simply, bacalao in olive oil and garlic. The cooking method, involving a constant shaking of the pan, produces a thick *ligado*, liaison sauce, from the collagen in the flesh of the fish.

**2 medium octopus, approximately
  500 g (1 lb 2 oz) each
1 bay leaf
10 black peppercorns
smoked or sweet paprika (pimentón),
  for sprinkling
2 tablespoons extra virgin olive oil
lemon wedges, to serve**

Serves 4

Wash the octopus. Using a small knife, carefully cut between the head and tentacles of the octopus, just below the eyes. Grasp the body of the octopus and push the beak out and up through the centre of the tentacles with your finger. Cut the eyes from the head of the octopus by slicing a small disc off with a sharp knife. Discard the eye section.

To clean the octopus head, carefully slit through one side (taking care not to break the ink sac) and scrape out any gut from inside. Rinse under running water to remove any remaining gut.

Bring a large saucepan of water to the boil. Add the bay leaf, peppercorns, 1 teaspoon salt and the octopus. Reduce the heat and simmer for 1 hour, or until tender. Remove the octopus from the water, drain well and leave for 10 minutes.

Cut the tentacles into 1 cm (½ inch) thick slices and cut the head into bite-sized pieces. Arrange on a serving platter and sprinkle with paprika and salt. Drizzle with the olive oil and garnish with lemon wedges.

pulpo gallego

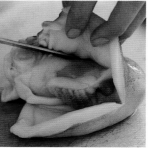

trout with jamón

**4 x 200 g (7 oz) river trout, cleaned
   and deboned**
**80 g (2¾ oz/1 bunch) mint, broken into
   sprigs**
185 ml (6 fl oz/¾ cup) white wine
8 slices jamón or prosciutto
2 tablespoons bacon fat
2 tablespoons lemon juice
40 g (1½ oz) chilled butter, chopped

Serves 4

Stuff each trout cavity with several sprigs of mint. Arrange in a dish in which they fit together snugly and drizzle with the wine. Cover and marinate in the refrigerator for at least 6 hours.

Preheat the oven to 180°C (350°F/Gas 4). Remove the fish from the marinade and pat dry, reserving the marinade. Remove the mint from each trout cavity and discard. Season the cavity. Roll up two pieces of jamón per fish and put in the cavity with some more mint sprigs.

Heat the bacon fat in a frying pan over medium heat for 4 minutes, or until melted. Add the fish and fry for 3 minutes each side, or until crisp. Transfer the fish to an ovenproof dish and bake for about 10 minutes, or until the fish is no longer translucent and can be flaked easily with a fork.

Meanwhile, combine the reserved marinade and lemon juice in the frying pan and boil over high heat for about 5 minutes, or until the sauce reduces to a syrupy consistency. Gradually whisk in the butter until the sauce is slightly glazy. Serve the fish with the jamón and mint inside, drizzled with the sauce.

20 large white scallops
60 g (2¼ oz) butter
2 tablespoons thinly sliced French shallots
375 ml (13 fl oz/1½ cups) cava or other
  sparkling white wine
250 ml (9 fl oz/1 cup) cream (whipping)
2–3 teaspoons lemon juice
1 tablespoon chopped flat-leaf (Italian)
  parsley

Serves 4

Remove and discard the vein, membrane or hard white muscle from the
scallops. Remove the roe.

Melt the butter in a large heavy-based frying pan over medium–high heat.
Sauté the scallops for 1–2 minutes each side, or until almost cooked through.
Transfer to a plate.

Add the shallots to the pan and cook for 3 minutes, or until soft. Add the
cava and simmer for 6–8 minutes, or until reduced by half. Stir in the cream
and simmer for about 10 minutes, or until reduced to a sauce consistency.
Stir in the lemon juice and season. Return the scallops to the sauce to reheat
gently, then serve garnished with the chopped parsley.

scallops with cava sauce

riches from the sea...

For many, Galicia in the country's north-western corner is the seafood capital of Spain. Here you'll find such culinary curiosities as *percebes* (goose barnacles). These delicious morsels, eaten raw or lightly boiled, look like miniature elephant's feet and are plucked from wave-lashed rocks by intrepid gatherers. And there are *navajas* (razor shell clams), named after the Spanish word for knife, which are delicious simply steamed.

Every day, fishing boats deliver fresh *langostas* and *bogavantes* (spiny lobsters and lobsters) and *buey*, the large crab named after the ox. All three are boiled in seawater by Galician cooks, served simply as a *mariscada* (seafood platter) with mayonnaise or *vinagreta*.

Everywhere you will find *pulpo gallego* (Galician octopus), boiled, cut into rings, drizzled with olive oil and dusted with *pimentón*, the Spanish version of paprika, and served on wooden plates.

Similar seafood, similarly treated, is to be found all along the Cantabrian coast, but special mention must be made of the *anchoas* (anchovies) of the Basque country when washed down with *chacoli*, the fresh white wine of Guetaria grown on the slopes overlooking the sea from which the fish come — a proximity that proves once and for all that God is a gastronome.

The Basques have given Spain the name for another culinary luxury: *kokotxas* (pronounced kokochas), a gelatinous triangle found in the jaw of all fish, but most delicious from the *merluza* (hake). They are usually fried and served with salsa verde, or simply with garlic.

In winter, all along the Atlantic coast, in estuaries and the mouths of rivers, wherever eels spawn, *angulas* (baby eels) are caught. This very expensive luxury is usually fried with garlic and dried capsicums (peppers), a dish known as *angulas a la bilbaina* (Bilbao-style baby eels).

But if we move into Catalonia and the Mediterranean, we'll find an altogether different kettle of fish on offer. Here, besides the seafood stew known as *zarzuela*, Catalans love simple *calamares a la plancha* (grilled calamari), *salmonetes al horno* (baked red mullet) or a *parillada de mariscos* (mixed grill of fish and/or shellfish). Dishes such as these are encountered along the whole coast.

Finally, in the southern-most province of Andalusia, you will find exquisitely fried fish (*pescaito frito*) being eaten in *freidurías* (street frying shops). The secret of the Andalusian frying technique? Large quantities of very hot olive oil. Try *filetes de merluza* (hake steaks), *acedías* (wedge sole), little fans of six anchovies tied by the tail, or *cazón* (dogfish marinated in vinegar, garlic and cumin before frying). Another speciality of the Mediterranean coast are the *cañaillas* (lightly boiled sea snails) and sweet *conquinas* (baby pippies), both of which are served as tapas.

baked bream with capsicum, chilli and potatoes

1.25 kg (2 lb 12 oz) whole red bream,
   red snapper or porgy, cleaned
1 lemon
60 ml (2 fl oz/¼ cup) olive oil
800 g (1 lb 12 oz) potatoes, thinly sliced
3 garlic cloves, thinly sliced
1 handful finely chopped flat-leaf (Italian)
   parsley
1 small red onion, thinly sliced
1 small dried red chilli, seeded and
   finely chopped

1 red capsicum (pepper), cored, seeded
   and cut into thin rings
1 yellow capsicum (pepper), cored,
   seeded and cut into thin rings
2 bay leaves
3–4 thyme sprigs
60 ml (2 fl oz/¼ cup) dry sherry

Serves 4–6

Cut off and discard the fins from the fish and put it in a large non-metallic dish. Cut two thin slices from one end of the lemon and reserve. Squeeze the juice from the rest of the lemon into the cavity of the fish. Add 2 tablespoons of the oil and refrigerate, covered, for 2 hours.

Preheat the oven to 190°C (375°F/Gas 5) and lightly oil a shallow earthenware baking dish large enough to hold the whole fish. Spread half the potatoes on the base and scatter the garlic, parsley, onion, chilli and capsicum on top. Season with salt and pepper. Cover with the rest of the potatoes. Pour in 80 ml (2½ fl oz/⅓ cup) water and sprinkle the remaining olive oil over the top. Cover with foil and bake for 1 hour.

Increase the oven temperature to 220°C (425°F/Gas 7). Season the fish inside and out with salt and pepper and put the bay leaves and thyme inside the cavity. Make three or four diagonal slashes on each side of the fish. Nestle the fish into the potatoes. Cut the reserved lemon slices in half and fit these into the slashes on one side of the fish, to resemble fins. Bake, uncovered, for 30 minutes, or until the fish is cooked through and the potatoes are golden and crusty.

Pour the dry sherry over the fish and return to the oven for 3 minutes. Serve straight from the dish.

500 g (1 lb 2 oz) small squid
2 tablespoons olive oil

PICADA
2 tablespoons extra virgin olive oil
2 tablespoons finely chopped flat-leaf
  (Italian) parsley
1 garlic clove, crushed

Serves 6

To clean the squid, gently pull the tentacles away from the tube (the intestines should come away at the same time). Remove the intestines from the tentacles by cutting under the eyes, then remove the beak if it remains in the centre of the tentacles by using your fingers to push up the centre. Pull away the soft bone from the hood.

Rub the tubes under cold running water. The skin should come away easily. Wash the hoods and tentacles and drain well. Transfer to a bowl, add ¼ teaspoon salt and mix well. Cover and refrigerate for 30 minutes.

Close to serving time, whisk the picada ingredients with ¼ teaspoon ground black pepper and some salt in a bowl.

Heat the oil in a frying pan over high heat and cook the squid hoods in small batches for 2–3 minutes, or until the hoods turn white and are tender. Cook the squid tentacles, turning to brown them all over, for 1 minute, or until they curl up. Serve hot, drizzled with the picada.

calamares a la plancha

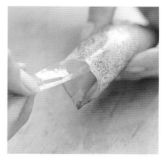

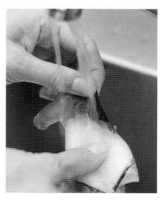

basque
seafood soup

1 tablespoon olive oil
1 carrot, finely diced
1 onion, finely diced
1 leek, finely diced
3 garlic cloves, chopped
1 small red chilli, seeded and finely chopped
1 celery stalk, finely diced
2 large all-purpose potatoes, peeled and cut into 2 cm (¾ inch) dice
500 g (1 lb 2 oz) skinless firm white fish fillets, cut into 2 cm (¾ inch) cubes, reserving any bones and scraps
1 bay leaf
250 ml (9 fl oz/1 cup) white wine

30 ml (1 fl oz) brandy
400 g (14 oz) tin chopped tomatoes, drained
60 ml (2 fl oz/¼ cup) tomato paste (concentrated purée)
12 black mussels, bearded and scrubbed
8 raw king prawns (shrimp), peeled and deveined, tails intact
2 tablespoons lemon juice
2 tablespoons chopped flat-leaf (Italian) parsley
allioli (page 250), to serve (optional)

Serves 4–6

Heat the oil in a large saucepan over medium heat. Add the carrot, onion, leek, garlic, chilli and celery and cook for 5 minutes, or until the onion is translucent. Add the potato and 1.5 litres (52 fl oz/6 cups) of cold water. Bring to the boil, then reduce the heat and simmer for about 8 minutes, or until the potatoes are half cooked. Stir in the fish bones and scraps and bay leaf and simmer for 6–8 minutes, or until the potatoes are soft. Strain the liquid and reserve. Remove the bones and bay leaf, and purée the remaining potato and vegetable mixture with the reserved liquid.

In a separate saucepan, combine the wine, brandy, diced tomato and tomato paste and bring to the boil. Add the mussels and cook, covered, for 3 minutes, or until opened. Remove from the pan, discarding any that remain closed.

Blend the mussel cooking liquid with the potato purée. Transfer to a large saucepan and bring to the boil. Add the fish pieces and prawns, reduce the heat and simmer for 8 minutes, or until all the seafood is cooked.

Stir in the mussels and lemon juice and gently heat through. Season well and garnish with the parsley. Delicious served with fried bread and allioli.

100 ml (3½ fl oz) sherry vinegar
80 ml (2½ fl oz/⅓ cup) olive oil
6 garlic cloves, crushed
1 small dried red chilli, seeded
   and chopped
2 tablespoons chopped flat-leaf
   (Italian) parsley
1 teaspoon sweet paprika (pimentón)
¼ teaspoon saffron threads
1 teaspoon dried oregano
80 ml (2½ fl oz/⅓ cup) vegetable oil
1 onion, chopped
1 leek, chopped
4 x 200 g (7 oz) skate fillets
lemon wedges, to serve

Serves 4

To make the dressing, put the vinegar in a small saucepan over high heat and bring to the boil. Boil for about 3 minutes, or until reduced by half. Leave to cool, then add the olive oil, half the garlic, the chopped chilli and a pinch of salt.

Meanwhile, combine the parsley, paprika, saffron threads and oregano in a mortar and pestle (or food processor) and grind to a paste.

Heat 2 tablespoons of the vegetable oil in a frying pan over medium heat and cook the spice paste, onion, leek and remaining garlic for 5 minutes, or until the onion and leek are translucent. Remove from the frying pan.

Heat the remaining vegetable oil in the pan, add the skate in batches and brown each side for 4–5 minutes, depending on the thickness of the fillets. Remove and cover with foil to keep warm. Return the onion and leek mixture to the frying pan and heat through.

Drizzle the dressing over the fish and serve with the onion and leek mixture spooned over the top. Garnish with lemon wedges.

skate with sherry vinegar

clams with white wine

1 kg (2 lb 4 oz) clams (vongole)
2 large ripe tomatoes
2 tablespoons olive oil
1 small onion, finely chopped
2 garlic cloves, crushed
1 tablespoon chopped flat-leaf
  (Italian) parsley
pinch of ground nutmeg
80 ml (2½ fl oz/⅓ cup) dry white wine

Serves 4

Soak the clams in salted water for 1 hour to release any grit. Rinse under running water and discard any open clams.

Score a cross in the base of each tomato. Place in a bowl of boiling water for 10 seconds, then plunge into cold water and peel away the skin from the cross. Cut the tomatoes in half and scoop out the seeds with a teaspoon. Finely chop the tomatoes.

Heat the oil in a large flameproof casserole dish and cook the onion over low heat for 5 minutes, or until softened. Add the garlic and tomato and cook for 5 minutes. Stir in the parsley and nutmeg and season with salt and pepper. Add 80 ml (2½ fl oz/⅓ cup) of water.

Add the clams and cook, covered, over low heat until they open (discard any that do not open). Add the wine and cook over low heat for 3–4 minutes, or until the sauce thickens, gently moving the dish back and forth a few times, rather than stirring, so that the clams stay in the shells. Serve immediately, with bread.

4 live large-bodied crabs
   (such as centollo or spider),
   about 750 g (1 lb 10 oz) each
80 ml (2½ fl oz/⅓ cup) olive oil
1 onion, finely chopped
1 garlic clove
125 ml (4 fl oz/½ cup) dry white wine
250 g (9 oz/1 cup) puréed tomato or
   tomato passata
¼ teaspoon finely chopped tarragon
2 tablespoons dry breadcrumbs
2 tablespoons chopped flat-leaf (Italian)
   parsley
40 g (1½ oz) chilled butter, chopped into
   small pieces

Serves 4

Bring a large saucepan of water to the boil. Stir in 3 tablespoons of salt, then add the crabs. Return to the boil and simmer, uncovered, for 15 minutes. Remove the crabs from the water and cool for 30 minutes. Extract the meat from the legs. Open the body without destroying the upper shell, which is needed for serving, reserving any liquid in a bowl. Take out the meat and chop finely with the leg meat. Scoop out all the brown paste from the shells and mix with the chopped meat.

Heat the olive oil in a frying pan over medium heat and cook the onion and garlic clove for 5–6 minutes, or until softened. Stir in the wine and puréed tomato. Simmer for 3–4 minutes, then add any reserved crab liquid. Simmer for a further 3–4 minutes. Add the crab meat and tarragon, and season with salt and ground black pepper. Simmer for about 5 minutes, or until thick. Discard the garlic.

Preheat the oven to 210°C (415°F/Gas 6–7). Rinse out and dry the crab shells. Spoon the crab mixture into the shells, levelling the surface. Combine the breadcrumbs and parsley and sprinkle over the top. Dot with butter and bake for 6–8 minutes, or until the butter melts and the breadcrumbs brown. Serve hot.

txangurro

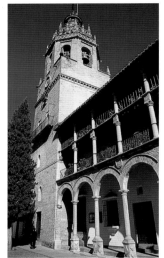

hake in green sauce

4 x 200 g (7 oz) hake steaks
seasoned plain (all-purpose) flour,
   for dusting
80 ml (2½ fl oz/⅓ cup) olive oil
3 garlic cloves, chopped
2 green chillies, seeded and chopped
125 ml (4 fl oz/½ cup) white wine
170 ml (5½ fl oz/⅔ cup) fish stock
1 large handful chopped flat-leaf (Italian)
   parsley
12 asparagus spears, lightly blanched and
   cut into 4 cm (1½ inch) lengths
60 g (2¼ oz/⅓ cup) cooked green peas

Serves 4

Dust the fish steaks with seasoned flour, shaking off any excess.

Heat the oil in a large frying pan over medium heat and cook the garlic and chilli for 1 minute, or until the garlic just starts to colour. Remove the chilli and garlic with a slotted spoon. Increase the heat to high and cook the hake for about 1 minute each side. Remove from the pan. Add the wine, stock, half the parsley and the garlic and chilli mixture to the pan and simmer until the sauce has thickened to your liking.

Add the fish, asparagus, peas and remaining parsley to the pan and simmer until the fish is cooked through. Serve immediately.

500 g (1 lb 2 oz) skinless firm white fish fillets (such as red mullet, whiting, redfish, garfish)
seasoned plain (all-purpose) flour, for dusting
100 ml (3½ fl oz) extra virgin olive oil
1 red onion, thinly sliced
2 garlic cloves, thinly sliced
2 thyme sprigs
1 teaspoon ground cumin
2 spring onions (scallions), finely chopped
½ teaspoon finely grated orange zest
60 ml (2 fl oz/¼ cup) fresh orange juice
185 ml (6 fl oz/¾ cup) white wine
185 ml (6 fl oz/¾ cup) white wine vinegar
60 g (2¼ oz) pitted green olives, roughly chopped
½ teaspoon caster (superfine) sugar

Serves 4

Dust the fish lightly with the seasoned flour, shaking off any excess.

Heat 2 tablespoons of the oil in a frying pan over medium heat and add the fish in batches. Cook the fish on both sides until lightly browned and just cooked through (the fish should flake easily when tested with a fork). Remove from the pan and put in a single layer in a large, shallow non-metallic dish.

Heat the remaining oil in the same pan, add the onion and garlic and cook, stirring, over medium heat for 5 minutes, or until soft.

Add the thyme, cumin and spring onion and stir until fragrant. Add the orange zest, orange juice, wine, vinegar, olives and sugar, and season with pepper, to taste. Bring to the boil and pour over the fish. Allow to cool in the liquid, then refrigerate overnight. Serve at room temperature.

escabeche

rice with stuffed squid

8 small squid, cleaned, tentacles reserved
1 small onion
2 tablespoons olive oil
2 tablespoons currants
2 tablespoons pine nuts
25 g (1 oz/⅓ cup) fresh breadcrumbs
1 tablespoon chopped mint
1 tablespoon chopped flat-leaf (Italian)
   parsley
1 egg, lightly beaten
2 teaspoons plain (all-purpose) flour

SAUCE
1 tablespoon olive oil
1 small onion, finely chopped
1 garlic clove, crushed
60 ml (2 fl oz/¼ cup) dry white wine
400 g (14 oz) tin chopped tomatoes

1 bay leaf
½ teaspoon sugar

RICE
1.25 litres (44 fl oz/5 cups) fish stock
60 ml (2 fl oz/¼ cup) olive oil
1 onion, finely chopped
3 garlic cloves, crushed
275 g (9¾ oz/1¼ cups) short-grain rice
¼ teaspoon cayenne pepper
3 teaspoons squid ink
60 ml (2 fl oz/¼ cup) dry white wine
60 ml (2 fl oz/¼ cup) tomato paste
   (concentrated purée)
2 tablespoons chopped flat-leaf (Italian)
   parsley

Serves 4

Finely chop the tentacles and onion in a processor. Heat the oil in a saucepan and cook the currants and pine nuts over low heat until the nuts are browned. Remove. Add the onion mix, cook gently for 5 minutes, then stir into the pine nut mixture with the breadcrumbs, herbs and egg. Season. Stuff into the squid bodies, close the openings and secure with toothpicks. Dust with flour.

To make the sauce, heat the oil in a frying pan and cook the onion over low heat until soft. Stir in the garlic, wine and 125 ml (4 fl oz/½ cup) of water. Cook over high heat for 1 minute, then add the tomato, bay leaf and sugar. Season, reduce the heat and simmer for 5 minutes. Add the squid to the pan in a single layer. Simmer, covered, for 20 minutes, or until tender.

To make the rice, bring the stock to a simmer in a saucepan. Heat the oil in a large saucepan and cook the onion over low heat until soft. Add the garlic, rice and cayenne. Mix the ink with 80 ml (2½ fl oz/⅓ cup) of stock, add to the rice with the wine and tomato paste and stir until the liquid has almost evaporated. Add 250 ml (9 fl oz/1 cup) of stock, simmer until this evaporates. Add the remaining stock, a cup at a time, until the rice is tender and creamy. Cover and leave off the heat for 5 minutes. Season. Stir in the parsley. Put the rice on a serving plate, arrange the squid on top and spoon on the sauce.

rice dishes... There is a story from Valencia, the home of paella, dating from the War of Independence fought against France (1808–1814). So impressed was a French general with the paella cooked by a local woman that he promised that for each new rice dish the woman cooked, he would free a Spanish prisoner of war. He was removed from his post after she had cooked 176 dishes — and she hadn't finished yet.

This anecdote is a polite Spanish way of saying there is more to Spanish rice dishes than paella which, you might be surprised to know, in its original form as *paella valenciana de la huerta* (Valencian paella from the vegetable garden) does not contain seafood.

Paella originated in the fertile coastal strip of the Ebro River delta region near Valencia. Its ingredients included rabbit, chicken, tomato, saffron, local dried and green beans and always, after that, controversy. Rosemary? No! Yes! Peas? Yes! No! There will always be debate in Valencia about the true ingredients of a paella.

Today, of course, we make paella with seafood. And why not? A cuisine that doesn't adapt and change ends up in a museum. But we should not forget the other remarkable rice dishes of Spain, including the classic Valencian *arroz con judias blancas y nabos* (rice with beans and turnips), which many claim as the greatest rice dish of all; or *arroz negro* (rice blackened with squid ink), also from Valencia; or *arroz al horno* (baked rice with chickpeas and garlic) from the Balearic Islands.

To make this multitude of rice dishes, there is a range of short-grained rice varieties, two of the most famous being *Calasparra* from the Murcian Segura River valley, which has a *Denominación de Origen* (DO), and the highly absorbent and nutty-flavoured *Bomba* from Valencia, a variety originally planted by the Moors.

30 raw large prawns (shrimp)
1 tablespoon olive oil

ROMESCO SAUCE
4 garlic cloves, unpeeled
1 roma (plum) tomato, halved and seeded
2 long red chillies
2 tablespoons whole blanched almonds
2 tablespoons hazelnuts
60 g (2¼ oz) sun-dried capsicums
   (peppers) in oil
1 tablespoon olive oil
1 tablespoon red wine vinegar

Serves 6–8

Peel the prawns, leaving the tails intact. Cut down the back and gently pull out the dark vein, starting at the head end. Mix the prawns with ¼ teaspoon of salt and refrigerate for 30 minutes.

To make the romesco sauce, preheat the oven to 200°C (400°F/Gas 6). Wrap the garlic cloves in foil, put on a baking tray with the tomato and chillies and bake for about 12 minutes. Spread the almonds and hazelnuts on the tray and bake for another 3–5 minutes. Leave to cool for 15 minutes.

Transfer the almonds and hazelnuts to a small blender or food processor and blend until finely ground. Squeeze the garlic and scrape the tomato flesh into the blender, discarding the skins. Split the chillies and remove the seeds. Scrape the flesh into the blender, discarding the skins. Pat the capsicums dry with paper towels, then chop them and add to the blender with the oil, vinegar, some salt and 2 tablespoons of water. Blend until smooth, adding more water, if necessary, to form a soft dipping consistency. Leave for 30 minutes.

Heat the olive oil in a frying pan over high heat and cook the prawns for 5 minutes, or until curled up and slightly pink. Serve with the sauce.

prawns with
romesco sauce

atún con tomate

4 x 200 g (7 oz) tuna steaks
80 ml (2½ fl oz/⅓ cup) lemon juice
2 tablespoons chopped flat-leaf
   (Italian) parsley
170 ml (5½ fl oz/⅔ cup) olive oil
1 onion, finely chopped
2 garlic cloves, chopped
400 g (14 oz) tin chopped tomatoes
1 bay leaf
1 teaspoon sugar
1 teaspoon chopped thyme
plain (all-purpose) flour, for dusting

Serves 4

Combine the tuna steaks with the lemon juice, half the parsley and a large pinch of salt, and leave to marinate for 15 minutes. Preheat the oven to 180°C (350°F/Gas 4).

Heat 80 ml (2½ fl oz/⅓ cup) of the oil in a saucepan over medium heat and cook the onion and garlic for 5 minutes, or until translucent. Add the tomato, bay leaf, sugar, thyme and remaining parsley, and season to taste. Increase the heat to high and cook for 3 minutes, or until some of the liquid has reduced.

Heat the remaining oil in a large frying pan over medium–high heat. Drain the tuna steaks and coat in the flour. Cook for about 3 minutes each side, or until golden, then transfer to a casserole dish. Cover with the tomato sauce and bake for 20 minutes, or until the tuna flakes easily.

1 kg (2 lb 4 oz) baby octopus
½ small red capsicum (pepper), seeded
125 g (4½ oz/⅓ cup) flaked almonds
3 garlic cloves, crushed
80 ml (2½ fl oz/⅓ cup) red wine vinegar
185 ml (6 fl oz/¾ cup) olive oil
2 tablespoons chopped flat-leaf (Italian)
    parsley

Serves 4

Using a small knife, carefully cut between the head and tentacles of the octopus and push the beak out and up through the centre of the tentacles using your fingers. Discard. To clean the octopus head, carefully slit through one side and pull out or chop out the gut. Rinse the octopus under running water. Drop the octopus into a large saucepan of boiling water and simmer for 20–40 minutes, depending on size, until tender. After 15 minutes cooking, start pricking them with a skewer to test for tenderness. When ready, remove from the heat and cool in the pan for 15 minutes.

To make the sauce, heat the grill (broiler) to high. Grill (broil) the capsicum, skin side up, until charred and blistered. Cool in a plastic bag. Peel away the skin, put in a food processor with the almonds and garlic, and purée. With the motor running, gradually pour in the vinegar followed by the oil. Stir in 125 ml (4 fl oz/½ cup) of boiling water and the parsley, and season to taste with salt and black pepper.

To serve, cut the tentacles into pieces. Put in a serving bowl with the sauce and toss to coat. Serve warm, or chill and serve as a salad.

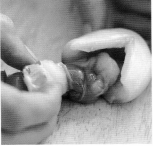

octopus in garlic almond sauce

marmitako

3 tablespoons olive oil
1 onion, diced
1 red capsicum (pepper), roughly diced
2 teaspoons sweet paprika (pimentón)
2 garlic cloves, finely chopped
2 bay leaves
250 g (9 oz/1 cup) tin chopped tomatoes
80 ml (2½ fl oz/⅓ cup) white wine
30 g (1 oz/¼ cup) capers, drained
650 g (1 lb 7 oz) all-purpose potatoes,
    peeled and cut into 1 cm (½ inch) slices

250 ml (9 fl oz/1 cup) chicken stock
4 x 200 g (7 oz) tuna steaks
1 small handful flat-leaf (Italian) parsley,
    chopped
1 tablespoon lemon juice
1 small red chilli, seeded and finely
    chopped (optional)

Serves 4

Preheat the oven to 180°C (350°F/Gas 4). Heat 2 tablespoons of the oil in a saucepan over medium heat and cook the onion, capsicum and paprika for 3 minutes, or until soft. Add the garlic, bay leaves and tomato and cook for 10 minutes. Stir in the wine and capers.

Meanwhile, arrange the potato slices in the bottom of a shallow 26 x 20 cm (10½ x 8 inch) casserole or heatproof dish. Spread the tomato and onion mixture over the potatoes and pour on the chicken stock. Bake in the oven for 40 minutes, or until the potatoes are almost cooked.

Season the tuna with salt and pepper and arrange on top of the potatoes. Bake for 5–8 minutes for rare or 10–15 minutes for medium. Season well and sprinkle the parsley, lemon juice and chilli over the top before serving.

a little taste of...

Home-style cooking. Let's admit it. We may admire Spain's new wave of cooking, *la nueva cocina*, lauded by many as the world's most exciting modern cuisine, but deep in the heart and not so deep in the palate lies a yearning for the earthy, gutsy and blatantly honest home cooking that you find from San Sebastián to Seville, from Barcelona to Badajoz. We should be grateful that what the Spanish people eat today is very much what they have eaten for hundreds of years: a bowl of *caldo gallego* on a winter's night in front of a warm fire with a glass of *rioja*, or a bowl of *ajo blanco* (often called white gazpacho) in the shade of a broad verandah in Seville with a glass of chilled *fino*. Picture the elegant simplicity of the Catalan classic *pato con peras* (duck with pears) with a glass of rich *garnacha* (grenache) from the Priorato region, or a lip-smacking rib-tickling gob-stopping *cocido madrileño*, not so much a dish as an entire meal, consisting of a soup and meat course, served separately — both, of course, with a glass of ink-black *tempranillo* from the Ribero del Duero.

...comida casera

gazpacho

1 kg (2 lb 4 oz) vine-ripened tomatoes
2 slices day-old white crusty bread,
  crusts removed, broken into pieces
1 red capsicum (pepper), seeded, roughly
  chopped
2 garlic cloves, chopped
1 small green chilli, chopped (optional)
1 teaspoon sugar
2 tablespoons red wine vinegar
2 tablespoons extra virgin olive oil

GARNISH
½ Lebanese (short) cucumber,
  seeded, finely diced
½ red capsicum (pepper), seeded,
  finely diced
½ green capsicum (pepper), seeded,
  finely diced
½ red onion, finely diced
½ ripe tomato, diced

Serves 4

Score a cross in the base of each tomato. Put in a bowl of boiling water for 10 seconds, then plunge into cold water and peel away the skin from the cross. Cut the tomatoes in half and scoop out the seeds with a teaspoon. Chop the tomatoes.

Soak the bread in cold water for 5 minutes, then squeeze out any excess liquid. Put the bread in a food processor with the tomato, capsicum, garlic, chilli, sugar and vinegar, and process until combined and smooth.

With the motor running, add the oil to make a smooth creamy mixture. Season to taste. Refrigerate for at least 2 hours. Add a little extra vinegar, if desired.

To make the garnish, mix together the ingredients. Spoon the chilled gazpacho into soup bowls, top with a little of the garnish and serve the remaining garnish in separate bowls on the side.

**200 g (7 oz) day-old white crusty bread,
   crusts removed**
**155 g (5½ oz/1 cup) whole blanched
   almonds**
3–4 garlic cloves, chopped
**125 ml (4 fl oz/½ cup) extra virgin
   olive oil**
**80 ml (2½ fl oz/⅓ cup) sherry or white
   wine vinegar**
**310–375 ml (10¾–13 fl oz/
   1¼–1½ cups) vegetable stock**
2 tablespoons olive oil
**75 g (2¾ oz) day-old white crusty bread,
   extra, crusts removed, cut into 1 cm
   (½ inch) cubes**
200 g (7 oz) small seedless green grapes

Serves 4–6

Soak the bread in cold water for 5 minutes, then squeeze out any excess liquid. Chop the almonds and garlic in a food processor until well ground. Add the bread and process until smooth.

With the motor running, add the oil in a steady slow stream until the mixture is the consistency of thick mayonnaise (add a little water if the mixture is too thick). Slowly add the sherry and 310 ml (10¾ fl oz/1¼ cups) of the stock. Blend for 1 minute. Season with salt. Refrigerate for at least 2 hours. The soup thickens on refrigeration so you may need to add stock or water to thin it.

When ready to serve, heat the olive oil in a frying pan, add the bread cubes and toss over medium heat for 2–3 minutes, or until golden. Drain on paper towels. Serve the soup very cold. Garnish with the grapes and bread cubes.

ajo blanco

caldo gallego

250 g (9 oz/1¼ cups) dried white
    haricot beans (such as navy beans)
500 g (1 lb 2 oz) smoked ham hock
2 tablespoons olive oil
1 leek, chopped
1 garlic clove, chopped
500 g (1 lb 2 oz) pork baby back or
    American-style ribs, separated into
    5 cm (2 inch) widths
2 all-purpose potatoes, peeled and cubed
1 bay leaf
1 kg (2 lb 4 oz/1 bunch) silverbeet (Swiss
    chard), washed well and chopped

Serves 4

Rinse the beans, then soak them in cold water for at least 5 hours. Put the ham hock in a large heavy-based saucepan and cover with cold water. Bring to the boil, then reduce the heat and simmer for about 1 hour, or until the meat starts to come away from the bone and is tender. Cool the hock. When the hock is cool enough to handle, remove the meat from the bone and cut into 2 cm (¾ inch) cubes. Reserve 625 ml (21½ fl oz/2½ cups) of the cooking liquid.

Meanwhile, put the beans in a large saucepan and cover with cold water. Bring to the boil, then reduce the heat and simmer for 30 minutes, or until tender. Drain, reserving 250 ml (9 fl oz/1 cup) of the cooking liquid.

Heat the olive oil in a large heavy-based saucepan over medium heat and cook the leek and garlic for about 5 minutes, or until translucent. Add the ham, beans, ribs, potato, bay leaf and reserved cooking liquid (make sure the food is covered with liquid).

Bring to the boil, then reduce the heat, cover and simmer for 45 minutes. Stir in the silverbeet and cook for a further 5 minutes. Season before serving.

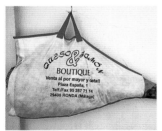

jamón and other smallgoods...

What is the difference between jamón and prosciutto? Most importantly, true jamón is made from the flesh of the Iberian pig, the famous *pata negra* (black foot, so named for its black coat), an animal whose recent revival has ensured the continuity of the magnificent *jamónes* of Spain.

The Iberian pig's natural habitat is the *dehesa*, sparse Mediterranean woodlands populated by oak and holm oak trees. Iberian hams—those made from the *pata negra*—include *Denominación de Origen* (DO) products from Jabugo, Teruel, Guijuelo, Dehesa de Extremadura and Huelva.

Serrano is the name given to any ham not made from the flesh of the *pata negra*, but from white-coated pigs, the best of these being *serrano consorcio* and *serrano especial*, and those from the town of Trevélez in the Alpujarras.

The second difference between jamón and prosciutto is the curing. Prosciutto is rubbed with salt, while jamón is packed in salt for several months, then hung and air-cured in the dry mountain air for 2, even 3 years. A slice of 3-year-old *Jabugo Gran Reserva* with a glass of old *amontillado* sherry is one of life's great food experiences.

Of course not all pork is turned into ham. Much of it is used in making *embutidos*—smallgoods of various sorts, cured and fresh. And this is where we come in contact with that other important ingredient in Spanish smallgoods, known in English by its Hungarian name, paprika.

The finest *pimentón* comes from La Vera in Extremadura in western Spain. Here, red capsicums (peppers) are dried, smoked and turned daily for 10–15 days over slow-burning holm oak fires. A chorizo spiced with La Vera *pimentón* will hold its colour for much longer.

There are countless regional smallgoods of Spain, the best known being chorizo, made of chopped or minced (ground) pork and either sweet or hot paprika (*pimentón*), garlic and black pepper. It is sold dried, for slicing and using as you would salami, or fresh for cooking in various dishes, most commonly with beans.

In Catalonia you will find *botifarra negra*, made of pig's blood, pork fat, some lean meat and mild seasonings, and *botifarra blanca*, a coarse white pork sausage seasoned with pepper.

Another blood pudding, *morcilla*, from Asturias, is made using pig's blood mixed with either rice or onion and often fennel, anise and pine nuts. It is an essential ingredient in *fabada*, the Asturian meat and bean stew.

Everywhere you will find *salchicha* (fresh pork sausage in links) and *salsichón*, as well as a hard, cured sausage called *longaniza* (or *fuet* if long and thin).

220 g (7¾ oz/1 cup) dried chickpeas
1 kg (2 lb 4 oz) chicken, trussed
500 g (1 lb 2 oz) beef brisket, in one piece
250 g (9 oz) piece smoke-cured bacon
125 g (4½ oz) tocino, streaky bacon
  or speck
1 pig's trotter
200 g (7 oz) chorizo
1 onion, studded with 2 cloves
1 bay leaf
1 morcilla blood sausage (optional)
250 g (9 oz) green beans, trimmed
  and sliced lengthways

250 g (9 oz) green cabbage, cut into
  sections through the heart
300 g (10½ oz) silverbeet (Swiss chard)
  leaves, washed well, stalks removed
4 small potatoes
2 leeks, cut into 10 cm (4 inch) lengths
pinch of saffron threads
75 g (2¾ oz) dried rice vermicelli

Serves 6–8

Soak the chickpeas in cold water overnight. Drain and rinse. Tie loosely in a muslin (cheesecloth) bag.

Put 3 litres (105 fl oz/12 cups) of cold water in a very large deep saucepan. Add the chicken, beef, bacon and tocino and bring to the boil. Add the chickpeas, pig's trotter and chorizo, return to the boil, then add the onion, bay leaf and ½ teaspoon salt. Simmer, partially covered, for 2½ hours (skim the surface if necessary).

After 2 hours, bring a saucepan of water to the boil, add the morcilla and gently boil for 5 minutes. Drain and set aside. Tie the green beans loosely in a muslin bag. Pour 1 litre (35 fl oz/4 cups) of water into the saucepan and bring to the boil. Add the cabbage, silverbeet, potatoes, leek and saffron with 1 teaspoon of salt. Return to the boil and simmer for 30 minutes. Add the green beans in the last 10 minutes of cooking.

Strain the stock from both the meat and vegetable pans and combine in a large saucepan. Bring to the boil, adjust the seasoning and stir in the vermicelli. Simmer for 6–7 minutes. Release the chickpeas and pile them in the centre of a large warm platter. Discard the tocino, then slice the meats and sausages. Arrange in groups around the chickpeas at one end of the platter. Release the beans. Arrange the vegetables in groups around the other end. Spoon a little of the simmering broth (minus the vermicelli) over the meat, then pour the rest into a soup tureen, along with the vermicelli. Serve at once. It is traditional to serve both dishes together, although the broth is eaten first.

cocido madrileño

pollo al chilindrón

6 ripe tomatoes
1.5 kg (3 lb 5 oz) chicken, cut into
    8 portions
60 ml (2 fl oz/¼ cup) olive oil
2 large red onions, cut into 5 mm (¼ inch)
    slices
2 garlic cloves, crushed
3 red capsicums (peppers), seeded,
    cut into 1 cm (½ inch) strips

60 g (2¼ oz) thickly sliced jamón
    or prosciutto, finely chopped
1 tablespoon chopped thyme
2 teaspoons sweet paprika (pimentón)
8 pitted black olives
8 pitted green olives

Serves 4

Score a cross in the base of each tomato. Put in a bowl of boiling water
for 10 seconds, then plunge into cold water and peel away the skin from
the cross. Cut each tomato in half and scoop out the seeds with a teaspoon.
Finely chop the flesh.

Pat dry the chicken with paper towels and season well with salt and pepper.
Heat the oil in a heavy-based frying pan over medium heat and cook the
chicken a few pieces at a time, skin side down, for 4–5 minutes, or until
golden. Turn the chicken over and cook for another 2–3 minutes. Transfer
to a plate.

Add the onion, garlic, capsicum, jamón and thyme to the frying pan. Cook,
stirring frequently, for 8–10 minutes, or until the vegetables have softened
but not browned.

Add the tomato and paprika, increase the heat and cook for 10–12 minutes,
or until the sauce has thickened and reduced. Return the chicken to the pan
and coat well with the sauce. Cover the pan and reduce the heat to low.
Simmer the chicken for 25–30 minutes, or until tender. Add the olives and
adjust the seasoning, if necessary, before serving.

80 ml (2½ fl oz/⅓ cup) olive oil
1 kg (2 lb 4 oz) lamb shoulder, diced
1 large onion, finely chopped
4 garlic cloves, crushed
2 teaspoons sweet paprika (pimentón)
100 ml (3½ fl oz) lemon juice
2 tablespoons chopped flat-leaf (Italian)
  parsley

Serves 4–6

Heat the oil in a large, heavy-based deep frying pan over high heat and
cook the lamb in two batches for 5 minutes each batch, or until well browned.
Remove all the lamb from the pan.

Add the onion to the pan and cook for 4–5 minutes, or until soft and golden.
Stir in the garlic and paprika and cook for 1 minute. Return the lamb to the
pan and add 80 ml (2½ fl oz/⅓ cup) of the lemon juice and 1.75 litres
(61 fl oz/7 cups) of water. Simmer over low heat, stirring occasionally, for
about 2 hours, or until the liquid has almost evaporated and the oil starts to
reappear. Stir in the parsley and remaining lemon juice, season with salt and
pepper, and serve.

cochifrito

tripe
with chickpeas

350 g (12 oz) dried chickpeas
800 g (1 lb 12 oz) honeycomb tripe, bleached and parboiled
170 ml (5½ fl oz/⅔ cup) olive oil
2 onions, chopped
6 garlic cloves, crushed
2 tablespoons sweet paprika (pimentón)
250 g (9 oz) chorizo, sliced
810 ml (28 fl oz/3¼ cups) white wine
400 g (14 oz) tin chopped tomatoes
2 tablespoons chopped thyme
2 tablespoons tomato paste (concentrated purée)

2 long green chillies, chopped
2 bay leaves
8 cloves
pinch of ground nutmeg
20 black peppercorns
200 g (7 oz) morcilla blood sausage, sliced
1 large handful flat-leaf (Italian) parsley, chopped

Serves 4

Soak the chickpeas overnight in cold water. Drain and rinse, then transfer to a saucepan and cover with fresh water. Bring to the boil over high heat and simmer for about 30 minutes, or until tender. Drain and rinse in cold water. Preheat the oven to 160°C (315°F/Gas 2–3).

Soak the tripe for 10 minutes, then rinse and drain. Cut into 5 cm (2 inch) squares. Heat the oil in a large flameproof casserole dish over medium heat and cook the onion and garlic for about 5 minutes, or until translucent. Stir in the tripe, paprika, chorizo and white wine. Bring to the boil and add the chopped tomato, thyme, tomato paste, chilli, bay leaves, cloves, nutmeg, peppercorns and salt, to taste. Stir in the blood sausage and cook, covered, in the oven for 1½–2 hours, or until the tripe is tender.

Remove the bay leaves from the casserole, add the chickpeas and cook, covered, for a further 10 minutes. Serve garnished with the parsley.

1.2 kg (2 lb 12 oz) chicken
½ lemon, cut into 2 wedges
2 bay leaves
60 ml (2 fl oz/¼ cup) olive oil
1 onion, thinly sliced
3 garlic cloves, crushed
400 g (14 oz) tin chopped tomatoes
170 ml (5½ fl oz/⅔ cup) white wine
2 tablespoons sun-dried tomato purée
   or tomato paste (concetrated purée)
1 red or green capsicum (pepper),
   cut into thin strips
40 g (1½ oz/⅓ cup) pitted black olives
3 tablespoons raisins
2 tablespoons pine nuts, toasted

Serves 4

Preheat the oven to 200°C (400°F/Gas 6). Wash and pat dry the chicken, then season with salt and pepper. Put the lemon wedges and bay leaves inside the cavity, drizzle with 2 tablespoons of the oil and roast in the oven for 1 hour. Pierce the chicken between the thigh and body through to the bone and check that the juices run out clear; if they are pink, cook for another 15 minutes.

Meanwhile, heat the remaining oil in a large frying pan over medium heat and cook the onion and garlic for 5 minutes, or until translucent. Add the tomato and cook for 2 minutes. Stir in the wine, tomato purée, capsicum, olives and raisins and simmer for 6–8 minutes, or until the mixture reaches a sauce consistency. Cut the chicken into eight portions, tipping the juice from the chicken cavity into the sauce. Spoon the sauce over the chicken and garnish with the pine nuts.

chicken with raisins and pine nuts

fideos a la catalana

80 ml (2½ fl oz/⅓ cup) olive oil
250 g (9 oz) pork spare ribs, cut into
  1 cm (½ inch) thick slices
1 onion, chopped
125 ml (4 fl oz/½ cup) puréed tomato
  or tomato passata
1 teaspoon sweet paprika (pimentón)
100 g (3½ oz) fresh spicy pork sausages,
  thickly sliced
100 g (3½ oz) chorizo, cut into pieces
1.5 litres (52 fl oz/6 cups) beef or chicken
  stock
500 g (1 lb 2 oz) spaghettini, broken into
  2.5 cm (1 inch) pieces

50 g (1¾ oz/⅓ cup) nuts (either
  hazelnuts, pine nuts or almonds)
2 garlic cloves, crushed
2 tablespoons chopped flat-leaf (Italian)
  parsley
¼ teaspoon ground cinnamon
1 slice bread, toasted and crusts removed
¼ teaspoon saffron threads

Serves 4–6

Heat the oil in a large heavy-based saucepan over medium–high heat and cook the ribs in batches until golden. Add the onion and cook for 5 minutes, or until softened. Stir in the puréed tomato and paprika and cook for a few minutes more.

Add the pork sausages, chorizo and the stock (reserving 2 tablespoons) and bring to the boil. Reduce to a simmer and add the spaghettini. Cook, covered, for 15 minutes, or until the pasta is *al dente*.

Meanwhile, in a mortar and pestle or food processor, crush the nuts with the garlic, parsley, cinnamon and bread to make a paste. Stir in the saffron. If the mixture is too dry, add 1–2 tablespoons of the reserved stock. Stir into the casserole and simmer for 5 minutes, or until the casserole has thickened slightly. Season well before serving.

**250 g (9 oz/1¼ cups) dried white haricot
  beans (such as navy beans)**
80 ml (2½ fl oz/⅓ cup) olive oil
2 garlic cloves, chopped
2 onions, chopped
1 teaspoon sweet paprika (pimentón)
1 teaspoon smoked paprika (pimentón)
2 teaspoons ground cumin
¼ teaspoon ground cinnamon
¼ teaspoon cayenne pepper
1 teaspoon dried rosemary
1 red capsicum (pepper), seeded and diced
**750 g (1 lb 10 oz) pork tenderloin,
  roughly diced**
400 g (14 oz) tin chopped tomatoes
250 ml (9 fl oz/1 cup) chicken stock
**300 g (10½ oz) orange sweet potato,
  peeled and roughly diced**
**60 g (2¼ oz) silverbeet (Swiss chard),
  washed well and shredded**

Serves 4

Cover the beans with cold water and soak for at least 3 hours. Drain well.
Preheat the oven to 160°C (315°F/Gas 2–3). Heat 2 tablespoons of oil in
a large saucepan over medium heat, add half the garlic and half the onion
and cook for 5 minutes, or until soft. Add the beans and cover with water.
Bring to the boil, then reduce the heat and simmer for 45 minutes, or until the
beans are soft but not mushy.

Meanwhile, heat the remaining oil in a large flameproof casserole dish over
medium heat. Add the remaining garlic and onion and cook for 5 minutes,
or until translucent. Stir in the spices, rosemary, capsicum and diced pork and
cook until the pork is evenly pale brown. Add the tomato and stock, bring to
the boil, then cover and cook in the oven for 1 hour. Add the beans and
sweet potato, top up with 250 ml (9 fl oz/1 cup) of water and return to the
oven for 30 minutes, or until the sweet potato is tender. Stir in the silverbeet
and cook for 5 minutes, or until the silverbeet is wilted. Season to taste.

gypsy stew

pato con peras

¼ teaspoon ground nutmeg
½ teaspoon smoked paprika (pimentón)
pinch of ground cloves
2 kg (4 lb 8 oz) duck, jointed into 8 pieces
1 tablespoon olive oil
1 bay leaf
8 French shallots, peeled
8 baby carrots, trimmed
2 garlic cloves, sliced
80 ml (2½ fl oz/⅓ cup) rich sweet
    sherry

1 thyme sprig
1 cinnamon stick
1.1 litres (38 fl oz) chicken stock
4 firm ripe pears, peeled, halved and cored
60 g (2¼ oz) whole almonds, toasted
25 g (1 oz) dark bittersweet chocolate,
    grated

Serves 4

Preheat the oven to 180°C (350°F/Gas 4). In a small bowl, mix together the nutmeg, paprika, cloves and a little salt and pepper. Dust the duck pieces with the spice mixture. Heat the oil in a large flameproof casserole dish and, when hot, brown the duck in batches. Remove from the dish.

Leaving a tablespoon of fat in the dish, drain off the excess. Add the bay leaf, shallots and carrots. Cook over medium heat for 3–4 minutes, or until lightly browned. Stir in the garlic and cook for a further 2 minutes. Pour in the sherry and boil for 1 minute to deglaze the casserole dish. Stir in the thyme, cinnamon stick and stock and return the duck to the dish.

Bring to the boil, then transfer the casserole to the oven and bake, covered, for 1 hour 10 minutes, turning halfway through. Put the pears on top of the duck and bake for a further 20 minutes.

Meanwhile, finely grind the almonds in a food processor, then combine with the chocolate.

When the duck is cooked, lift the duck pieces and the pears out of the liquid using a slotted spoon and transfer to a serving dish with the carrots, shallots and cinnamon stick. Keep warm.

Put the casserole dish on the stovetop over medium heat and bring the liquid to the boil. Boil for 7–10 minutes, or until the liquid has reduced by half. Add 60 ml (2 fl oz/¼ cup) of the hot liquid to the ground almonds and chocolate and stir to combine. Whisk the paste into the rest of the sauce to thicken. Season to taste, pour over the duck and serve.

250 g (9 oz) dried chickpeas, soaked
    in water overnight
1 carrot, diced
1 flat-leaf (Italian) parsley sprig
1 bay leaf
2 onions, chopped
80 ml (2½ fl oz/⅓ cup) extra virgin
    olive oil
1 garlic clove, chopped
2 tomatoes, chopped
250 g (9 oz) silverbeet (Swiss chard),
    washed well and chopped
2 hard-boiled eggs, peeled and chopped

Serves 4

Drain and rinse the chickpeas and put in a large saucepan with the carrot, parsley, bay leaf and half the onion. Cover with 750 ml (26 fl oz/3 cups) of water, bring to the boil and cook for about 20 minutes, or until almost tender. Add 2 teaspoons of salt and half the oil and cook for 10 minutes.

Heat the remaining oil in a frying pan and cook the garlic and remaining onion. Add the tomato and cook for 5 minutes. Stir the tomato mixture and silverbeet into the chickpea mixture (it should be wet enough to be saucy but not too soupy). Cook for 5 minutes, or until the silverbeet is tender. Season well and serve garnished with the boiled egg.

chickpeas and silverbeet

pollo a la cerveza

350 ml (12 fl oz) bottle of beer
   (Spanish or Mexican if possible)
1 tablespoon dijon mustard
1 teaspoon sweet paprika (pimentón)
1 onion, diced
1 garlic clove, crushed
1.2 kg (2 lb 12 oz) chicken, cut into pieces
2 tablespoons olive oil
1 green capsicum (pepper), diced
400 g (14 oz) tin chopped tomatoes
1 onion, extra, diced
1 garlic clove, extra, crushed

Serves 4

Combine the beer, mustard, paprika, half the onion, half the garlic and a large pinch of salt in a large bowl. Add the chicken, toss until well coated and marinate overnight in the refrigerator.

Preheat the oven to 180°C (350°F/Gas 4). Heat the olive oil in a large flameproof casserole dish over medium heat, add the capsicum and extra onion and garlic and cook for 10 minutes, or until softened.

Stir in the chicken, marinade and tomato and season well. Cover and bake for 45–60 minutes, or until the chicken is tender.

mountain food...
Turn your back on the teeming cities and tourist towns along the coast, and head for the hills to discover a surprising truth. No country in Europe has so much wilderness, and so many rugged mountain ranges.

For example, in Asturias the Picos de Europa, Europe's largest national park, only 15 kilometres (9.3 miles) from the coast, is a mountain range comprising three towering massifs, divided by deep gorges. Meandering through the Picos are cold, clear rivers filled with trout and salmon in season, and villages still so remote as to be cut off from car access.

So wild is this region that wolves are a continuing problem for livestock farmers. The wolf is protected, but if a wolf kills a sheep or a goat, then the farmer can be compensated — if he can prove that the stock was killed in the national park. We understand many dead sheep have been dragged into the national park in the dead of night.

Half an hour from Madrid begins the Sierra de Guadarrama; behind Gerona, the mountains of the Cantabrian Range; and south of Granada, the Sierra Nevada, with the highest mountains in Europe, reaching 3500 metres (11 480 feet). Driving along these precipitous mountain roads, you see a sign on many farm gates: *coto de caza* (hunting reserve). In these private reserves, men hunt partridge, pheasant, woodcock, hare and wild boar. And not just for the sport, but also for the table. The Spanish repertoire is heavy with recipes for game, such as *morteruelo* (partridge and hare stew) and *codornices con aceitunas* (quail with olives).

And not just animals are hunted in those mountain passes. The damp forests of Galicia, Navarra and the Basque country are alive with wild mushrooms in season. You'll find an abundance of morels, chanterelles and ceps, all with local names.

Mountain dishes are different even when the ingredients are not hunted. Clambering up and down all day creates gargantuan appetites, and dishes to satisfy them. Your first proper *fabada asturiana* (a stew of the local fava beans, chorizo, morcilla, pig's ear and hocks, eaten in the Picos) will leave you stunned and, well, stuffed.

And all jokes aside — and we've heard plenty of them — if you really love your beef, seek out the restaurants near the bull rings that specialize in cuts of fighting bulls. Once there, you must try the famous stew, *rabo de toro*. And yes, you can eat the testicles, deep-fried.

300 g (10½ oz) green beans, trimmed
1 tablespoon olive oil
1 onion, finely chopped
2 garlic cloves, finely chopped
1 tablespoon sweet paprika (pimentón)
¼ teaspoon chilli flakes
1 bay leaf, crushed
400 g (14 oz) tin chopped tomatoes
2 tablespoons chopped flat-leaf (Italian)
   parsley

Serves 4

Cook the beans in boiling water for 3–5 minutes, or until tender. Drain and set aside.

Heat the olive oil in a frying pan, add the onion and cook over medium heat for 5 minutes, or until soft. Add the garlic and cook for 1 minute. Add the paprika, chilli flakes and bay leaf, cook for 1 minute, then stir in the tomato. Simmer over medium heat for 15 minutes, or until reduced and pulpy. Add the beans and parsley and cook for 1 minute, or until warmed through. Season to taste. Serve warm or at room temperature.

judias verdes
en salsa de tomate

lamb caldereta

2 tablespoons olive oil
1 onion, roughly diced
1 carrot, roughly diced
1 red capsicum (pepper), cut into large dice
2 garlic cloves, chopped
1 kg (2 lb 4 oz) lamb leg, boned and cut
    into 2 cm (¾ inch) cubes
1 ham bone or trimmings
400 g (14 oz) tin chopped tomatoes
2 tablespoons chopped flat-leaf (Italian)
    parsley
2 tablespoons chopped mint
2 tablespoons tomato paste (concentrated
    purée)
2 bay leaves
250 ml (9 fl oz/1 cup) white wine
1 teaspoon ground cumin
1 teaspoon sweet paprika (pimentón)
25 g (1 oz/¼ cup) dry breadcrumbs
½ teaspoon ground cinnamon

Serves 4

Preheat the oven to 180°C (350°F/Gas 4). Heat the olive oil in a large flameproof casserole dish over medium heat and cook the onion, carrot, capsicum and garlic until softened. Add the lamb cubes, ham bone or trimmings, tomato, parsley, mint, tomato paste, bay leaves, white wine and 185 ml (6 fl oz/¾ cup) of water. Bring to the boil, then cover and bake for 1–1½ hours, or until the lamb is tender.

Meanwhile, combine the cumin, paprika, breadcrumbs, cinnamon and a pinch of pepper.

Remove the lamb from the casserole dish with a slotted spoon or tongs and set aside. Discard the bay leaves and ham bone. Purée the remaining liquid and vegetables, then stir in the breadcrumb mixture. Cook, stirring, for about 10 minutes, or until the sauce has thickened. Return the lamb to the casserole and gently warm through. Serve with green beans.

400 g (14 oz) green lentils
100 ml (3½ fl oz) olive oil
2 garlic cloves, crushed
1 green capsicum (pepper), seeded
  and diced
2 onions, chopped
2 teaspoons sweet paprika (pimentón)
1 bay leaf
2 slices bacon, cut into thin strips
200 g (7 oz) chorizo, sliced
1 tomato, chopped
extra virgin olive oil, for drizzling

Serves 4

Rinse the lentils, then cover with cold water and soak for 2 hours.

Heat 1 tablespoon of the olive oil in a large saucepan over medium heat and cook the garlic, capsicum and half the onion for 5 minutes, or until the onion is translucent. Add the drained lentils, paprika, bay leaf and most of the remaining oil. Cover with water, bring to the boil, then reduce the heat and simmer for 30 minutes, or until tender.

Meanwhile, heat the remaining oil in a frying pan. Add the bacon, chorizo and remaining onion and fry until golden. Add to the lentil mixture with the tomato and a large pinch of salt, and cook for another 5 minutes. Drizzle a little extra virgin olive oil over the top and serve.

stewed lentils with chorizo

rabbit in red wine

2 x 1 kg (2 lb 4 oz) rabbits, jointed
and cut into 8 pieces each
100 ml (3½ fl oz) olive oil
1 large onion, chopped
6 roma (plum) tomatoes, peeled
and chopped
1 teaspoon sweet paprika (pimentón)
6 garlic cloves, crushed
3 slices jamón or prosciutto, cut into strips
100 g (3½ oz) chorizo, chopped
3 red capsicums (peppers), seeded
and diced
2 tablespoons chopped thyme
250 ml (9 fl oz/1 cup) red wine
1 handful chopped flat-leaf
(Italian) parsley

Serves 4

Season the rabbit pieces. Heat half the oil in a heavy-based flameproof casserole dish over medium heat, add the rabbit in batches and cook for about 4 minutes per batch, or until golden brown. Remove and set aside.

Heat the rest of the oil in the dish and cook the onion for 5 minutes, or until translucent. Add the tomato and simmer gently for 10 minutes. Stir in the paprika, garlic, jamón, chorizo, capsicum, thyme, red wine, rabbit pieces and 2 tablespoons of the parsley. Check the seasoning. Bring to the boil, then reduce the heat and simmer for 35 minutes, or until the rabbit is tender.

Remove the rabbit pieces and simmer the sauce for 20–30 minutes, or until reduced and glazy. Return the rabbit to the casserole and gently heat through. Season to taste, garnish with the remaining parsley and serve.

60 ml (2 fl oz/¼ cup) olive oil
40 g (1½ oz/¼ cup) pine nuts
1 thick slice bread, crusts removed,
    cut into pieces
½ teaspoon ground cinnamon
pinch of saffron threads
2 garlic cloves
2 tablespoons chopped flat-leaf (Italian)
    parsley
1.5 kg (3 lb 5 oz) chicken, cut into 8 pieces
    and seasoned with salt

2 onions, finely chopped
125 ml (4 fl oz/½ cup) white wine
375 ml (13 fl oz/1½ cups) chicken stock
1 bay leaf
2 thyme sprigs
2 tablespoons lemon juice
2 egg yolks

Serves 4

Heat 1 tablespoon of the oil in a heavy-based flameproof casserole dish over medium–high heat. Add the pine nuts and bread and fry for 3 minutes, or until golden. Remove and drain on paper towels. When cooled slightly, put in a mortar and pestle or food processor, add the cinnamon, saffron, garlic and half the parsley, and grind or process to a coarse, crumbly consistency.

Heat the rest of the oil in the casserole dish over medium heat and brown the chicken pieces for about 5 minutes. Remove to a plate. Add the onion and cook gently for 5 minutes, or until translucent.

Return the chicken pieces to the casserole dish with the wine, stock, bay leaf and thyme and simmer, covered, over medium heat for 1 hour, or until the chicken is tender. Remove the chicken and cover to keep warm. Add the pine nut paste to the dish and cook for 1 minute. Remove from the heat and whisk in the lemon juice, egg yolks and remaining parsley. Return the casserole dish to the stovetop and stir over very low heat until just thickened slightly (do not allow it to boil or the sauce will split). Season to taste, return the chicken to the casserole and gently warm through before serving.

chicken in saffron stew

oxtail stew

2 kg (4 lb 8 oz) oxtails, cut into
   2 cm (¾ inch) thick pieces
seasoned plain (all-purpose) flour,
   for dusting
80 ml (2½ fl oz/⅓ cup) olive oil
2 onions, chopped
1 leek, diced
2 carrots, diced
1 celery stalk, chopped
2 garlic cloves, crushed
400 g (14 oz) tin chopped tomatoes
375 ml (13 fl oz/1½ cups) white wine
375 ml (13 fl oz/1½ cups) beef stock
1 teaspoon sweet paprika (pimentón)
1 bay leaf
2 tablespoons chopped thyme
2 tablespoons chopped flat-leaf (Italian)
   parsley

Serves 4–6

Preheat the oven to 150°C (300°F/Gas 2). Coat the oxtails with seasoned flour. Heat 2 tablespoons of oil in a large, heavy-based flameproof casserole dish over medium heat and brown the oxtails in batches. Remove to a plate.

Heat the remaining oil in the casserole dish over medium heat, add the onion, leek, carrot, celery and garlic and cook for 5 minutes, or until the vegetables are softened.

Stir in the tomato, white wine, stock, paprika, bay leaf and thyme and bring to the boil. Add the oxtails, making sure they are covered in liquid (add extra water if necessary), then cover and bake for 4–5 hours, depending on the size of the tails. The meat should easily fall away from the bone when ready. Serve garnished with chopped parsley.

500 g (1 lb 2 oz) bacalao (salt cod)
2 tablespoons olive oil
1 onion, chopped
2 garlic cloves, finely chopped
400 g (14 oz) tin chopped tomatoes
½ teaspoon sweet paprika (pimentón)
½ teaspoon smoked paprika (pimentón)
pinch of saffron threads
10 black peppercorns
1 teaspoon cumin seeds

500 ml (17 fl oz/2 cups) chicken stock
100 g (3½ oz) dried lasagne sheets, cut
   in half to form squares approximately
   9 x 9 cm (3½ x 3½ inches)
2 tablespoons chopped flat-leaf (Italian)
   parsley
1 tablespoon lemon juice

Serves 4

Soak the bacalao in plenty of cold water for about 20 hours, changing the water four or five times to remove excess saltiness.

Drain, then put the bacalao in a large saucepan and cover with cold water. Bring to the boil, then reduce the heat and simmer for 20 minutes, or until the fish is soft and able to be removed from the bone. Drain, allow to cool, then shred the bacalao.

Heat the oil in a large, heavy-based flameproof casserole dish over medium heat. Cook the onion and garlic for about 5 minutes, or until translucent. Add the crushed tomatoes and cook for 2 minutes. Stir in the sweet and smoked paprika and the shredded fish.

In a mortar and pestle or food processor, grind the saffron, peppercorns and cumin seeds to a powder. Add to the casserole with the chicken stock and simmer for 15 minutes, or until reduced to a sauce consistency.

Meanwhile, cook the lasagne sheets in boiling water until *al dente*. Stir into the casserole and season to taste. Garnish with the parsley, drizzle the lemon juice over the top and serve.

tatters and rags

wine, cider and beer...

Spanish wines have been dubbed 'postmodern'. Perhaps because, of all the old world wine countries, the Spanish have been the most nimble in adopting new techniques and new flavours, and the last to abandon the traditional methods that continue to work.

Today, Spanish wines span the centuries. An indigenous variety like *verdejo*, which normally oxidized so fast it was only used to make *rancio* wines (wines such as sherry in which the oxidation was controlled) now produce fresh table wines under inert gas. At the same time, other winemakers are returning to the ancient methods and making wines in large concrete vats reminiscent of the terracotta *tinajas* used in ancient times.

This coexistence of technology and tradition, and the wide variety of soils, sites and microclimates, results in a remarkable range of wines of exceptional quality, from the timeless sherries and wines made using indigenous Spanish varieties (*tempranillo*, *albariño* and *negramoll*, for example) to rich and powerful wines made using the French varieties cabernet sauvignon and chardonnay.

In addition, there are the incomparable cavas or sparkling wines of Catalonia, made using the *método tradicional* by large and small winemakers — and worth a book of their own.

A new region of great interest to wine lovers is Navarra, which produces rich red wines from *tempranillo* and *garnacha* (grenache) grapes, and also firm and fruity *rosados* (rosés), also from *garnacha*.

No words on Spanish wine can be complete without mentioning the majestic wines from the house of Vega Sicilia at Valbuena in Ribero del Duero. Should you be offered a glass of the *Unica Vega Sicilia Reserva Especial*, you will know you are an honoured guest indeed.

And then there is *sidra*, the cider of northern Spain, drunk in large cider houses from the Basque country all the way to Galicia, and poured with great ceremony and dexterity into large thin glass tumblers from a great height to aerate it. You will either love or hate this powerful and sour drink, which has a cult following in what is known as 'green Spain', the cold and mountainous north.

Finally, *cerveza* (or beer), a word derived from Ceres, the Roman goddess of the harvest. Many a foreigner has survived for weeks on end in Spain with the phrase *una cerveza por favor* (a beer please) as their only words of Spanish. And you will find some very fine beers in Spain, mainly pilsener style, all of which go down extremely well with tapas.

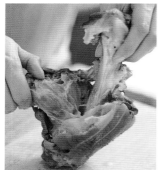

fabada asturiana

**400 g (14 oz) dried white haricot beans
   (such as navy beans)**
700 g (1 lb 9 oz) smoked ham hock
2 tablespoons olive oil
150 g (5½ oz) bacon, chopped
1 onion, chopped
2 garlic cloves, chopped
pinch of saffron threads
1 teaspoon sweet paprika (pimentón)
1 bay leaf
**200 g (7 oz) morcilla blood sausages,
   sliced**

Serves 4

Rinse the beans and soak overnight in cold water.

Put the ham hock in a large saucepan and cover with water. Bring to the boil, then reduce the heat and simmer for at least 1 hour, or until the meat is tender and starting to come away from the bone. Allow to cool, then remove the meat from the bone and cut into 2 cm (¾ inch) cubes. Reserve 1 litre (35 fl oz/4 cups) of the cooking liquid.

Heat the oil in a large heavy-based saucepan and cook the bacon, onion and garlic for 5 minutes, or until translucent. Add the beans, cubed ham, saffron, paprika and bay leaf, and season to taste.

Add the reserved cooking liquid, bring to the boil, then reduce the heat and simmer for at least 1 hour, or until the beans are cooked (they should be soft but not mushy). Add the blood sausage and cook for 5 minutes, or until heated through. Season before serving.

1.5 kg (3 lb 5 oz) chicken, cut into 8 pieces
60 ml (2 fl oz/¼ cup) olive oil
2 large onions, chopped
400 g (14 oz) eggplant (aubergine),
    peeled and cut into 2 cm (¾ inch) cubes
3 garlic cloves, crushed
350 g (12 oz) zucchini (courgettes), cut
    into strips
2 green or red capsicums (peppers), cut
    into 1 cm (½ inch) strips
2 x 400 g (14 oz) tins chopped tomatoes
1 bay leaf
2 tablespoons chopped herbs (such as
    thyme, oregano and flat-leaf (Italian)
    parsley)
125 ml (4 fl oz/½ cup) white wine

Serves 4

Season the chicken pieces with salt and pepper. Heat the oil in a large heavy-based saucepan over medium heat, add the chicken in batches and brown well on all sides. Remove from the pan and reduce the heat to medium–low.

Add the onion and cook for about 10 minutes, or until translucent. Add the eggplant, garlic, zucchini and capsicum and cook for 10 minutes, or until the vegetables are softened.

Stir in the tomato, bay leaf, herbs and wine, and return the chicken pieces to the pan. Bring to the boil, then cover and simmer over low heat for about 45 minutes, or until the chicken is tender and the eggplant is soft. Season well with salt and pepper before serving.

chicken samfaina

silverbeet with
raisins and pine nuts

500 g (1 lb 2 oz) silverbeet (Swiss chard)
  or English spinach
2 tablespoons pine nuts
1 tablespoon olive oil
1 small red onion, halved and sliced
1 garlic clove, thinly sliced
2 tablespoons raisins
pinch of ground cinnamon

Serves 6

Trim the stalks from the silverbeet, then wash the leaves and shred them.

Put the pine nuts in a frying pan and stir over medium heat for 3 minutes, or until lightly brown. Remove from the pan.

Heat the oil in the pan, add the onion and cook over low heat, stirring occasionally, for 10 minutes, or until translucent. Increase the heat to medium, add the garlic and cook for 1 minute. Add the silverbeet with the water clinging to it, the raisins and cinnamon. Cover and cook for 2 minutes, or until the silverbeet wilts. Stir in the pine nuts, season to taste and serve.

1 red onion
6 small eggplants (aubergines),
    about 16 cm (6¼ inches) long
4 red capsicums (peppers)
4 orange capsicums (peppers)
1 tablespoon baby capers, rinsed and
    drained
80 ml (2½ fl oz / ⅓ cup) olive oil
1 tablespoon chopped flat-leaf (Italian)
    parsley
2 garlic cloves, finely chopped

Serves 4

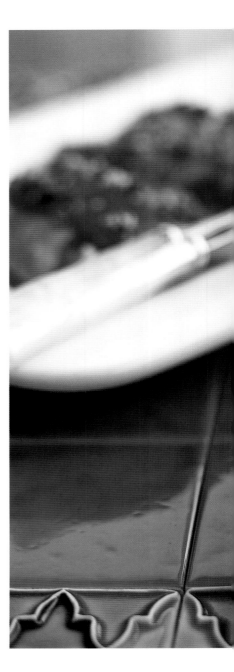

Without slicing through the base, cut the red onion from top to bottom into six sections, leaving it attached at the base. Put on a barbecue, or over an open-flamed grill or gas stovetop with the eggplants and capsicums. Cook over medium heat for 10 minutes, turning occasionally, until the eggplant and capsicum skins are blackened and blistered. Put the capsicums in a plastic bag for 10 minutes to cool. Set aside the onion and eggplant.

Dry-fry the capers with a pinch of salt until crisp. Cut the onion into its six sections and discard the charred outer skins. Peel the skins off the eggplants and remove the stalks. Cut the eggplants from top to bottom into slices. Peel the capsicums and remove the seeds. Cut the capsicums into wide slices. Arrange all the vegetables on a large serving platter. Drizzle the olive oil over the top and season with salt and pepper. Scatter the parsley, garlic and capers over the top. Serve cold as a salad or warm as an accompaniment to barbecued meats.

escalivada

quails in vine leaves

8 quails
2 lemons
8 slices jamón or prosciutto
16 vine leaves in brine, rinsed in
  cold water
1 tablespoon olive oil
60 ml (2 fl oz/¼ cup) veal or chicken
  stock
100 ml (3½ fl oz) sweet sherry
50 g (1¾ oz) chilled butter, diced
250 g (9 oz) watercress, picked over

Serves 4

Preheat the oven to 200°C (400°F/Gas 6). Wash the quails and pat dry with paper towels. Cut the lemons into quarters and put a quarter inside each quail cavity. Season and wrap each quail with a slice of jamón. Put a quail on top of two overlapping vine leaves, fold the leaves around the bird and secure with kitchen twine. Repeat with the remaining quails and leaves.

Put the wrapped quails in a roasting tin, drizzle with the oil and bake for 30 minutes. Remove from the oven and pierce one bird between the thigh and body through to the bone and check that the juices run out clear. If they are pink, cook for another 5 minutes. Transfer the quails to a separate plate to rest for 10 minutes, removing the twine and vine leaves.

Pour the remaining juices in the roasting tin into a small saucepan and add the stock and sherry. Bring to the boil and gradually whisk in the butter for 3 minutes, or until the sauce is slightly glazy. Serve the quail on a bed of watercress, drizzled with the sauce.

1.5 kg (3 lb 5 oz) lamb leg
2 tablespoons olive oil
250 ml (9 fl oz/1 cup) white wine
150 g (5½ oz/1 bunch) flat-leaf (Italian)
   parsley, chopped
2 teaspoons finely chopped rosemary
2 teaspoons finely chopped thyme
8 garlic cloves, crushed

Serves 4

Preheat the oven to 200°C (400°F/Gas 6). Rinse the lamb leg and pat dry with paper towels. Put the lamb in a roasting tin and drizzle the olive oil and wine over the top. Mix together the parsley, rosemary, thyme and garlic and sprinkle over the lamb, pressing down firmly.

Put the lamb in the oven and cook for 20 minutes, basting with the juices in the tin. Reduce the temperature to 180°C (350°F/Gas 4) and cook for 1 hour. Remove from the oven and rest for at least 10 minutes before serving. The lamb will be medium–rare to medium. If you prefer your lamb to be rare, allow 20–25 minutes cooking time per 500 g (1 lb 2 oz), and for well done, 30–35 minutes per 500 g (1 lb 2 oz).

roast leg of lamb

pimientos rellenos

4 red capsicums (peppers)
60 ml (2 fl oz/¼ cup) olive oil
1 onion, chopped
2 garlic cloves, chopped
400 g (14 oz) minced (ground) pork
   or beef
125 ml (4 fl oz/½ cup) white wine
400 g (14 oz) tin chopped tomatoes,
   drained well
100 g (3½ oz) rice, cooked
1 egg, lightly beaten
2 tablespoons finely chopped flat-leaf
   (Italian) parsley

Serves 4

Cut the tops off the capsicums and reserve them to use as lids. Using a small, sharp knife, carefully cut the internal membrane and seeds away from the capsicum and discard. Preheat the oven to 180°C (350°F/Gas 4).

Heat 2 tablespoons of the olive oil in a frying pan over medium–high heat and cook the onion and garlic for 5 minutes, or until lightly golden. Add the pork or beef and brown well. Stir in the wine, then reduce the heat to low and simmer for about 10 minutes, or until the wine has been absorbed.

Add the tomato and simmer for a further 10 minutes, then add the rice. Remove from the heat and stir in the beaten egg and parsley. Season well.

Stuff the capsicums with the meat mixture, put the lids on top and stand upright in an ovenproof dish. Drizzle with the remaining olive oil and bake for 45–50 minutes, or until the stuffing is cooked through and the capsicums are tender. Remove from the oven and leave, covered, for about 5 minutes before serving.

2 tablespoons olive oil
125 g (4½ oz) minced (ground) beef
125 g (4½ oz) minced (ground) pork
200 g (7 oz) chicken livers, chopped
1 onion, diced
1 leek, halved lengthways and chopped
2½ tablespoons dry sherry
1 tablespoon chopped thyme
400 g (14 oz) tin chopped tomatoes
4 tablespoons chopped flat-leaf (Italian)
   parsley
75 g (2¾ oz) butter

60 g (2¼ oz/½ cup) plain (all-purpose)
   flour
1 litre (35 fl oz/4 cups) milk
pinch of ground nutmeg
250 g (9 oz) packet dried cannelloni
   tubes
100 ml (3½ fl oz) puréed tomato or
   tomato passata
100 g (3½ oz/1 cup) grated Manchego or
   Parmesan cheese

Serves 6

Preheat the oven to 180°C (350°F/Gas 4). Heat the olive oil in a large heavy-based frying pan over medium heat. Cook the beef, pork, chicken livers, onion and leek for 10 minutes, or until well browned, breaking up any lumps with the back of a wooden spoon. Add the sherry, thyme, tomato and half the parsley and cook for 3 minutes, or until most of the liquid has evaporated. Season and leave to cool.

To make the white sauce, melt the butter in a large saucepan over medium heat. Add the flour and cook, stirring with a wooden spoon, for 1–2 minutes, or until pale yellow. Remove from the heat and add the milk gradually, stirring constantly until blended. Return to the heat and slowly bring the mixture to the boil, whisking for 15 minutes, or until thickened. Season with nutmeg, salt and pepper.

Fill the cannelloni with the meat mixture using a wide-tip piping bag or a spoon. Put the filled cannelloni side by side in a buttered ovenproof dish. Pour the white sauce over the top and dot with the puréed tomato. Top with the grated cheese and bake for 40–45 minutes. Garnish with the remaining chopped parsley.

catalan-style cannelloni

tumbet

TOMATO SAUCE
1 kg (2 lb 4 oz) ripe tomatoes
2 tablespoons olive oil
3 garlic cloves, crushed
1 red onion, finely chopped
2 teaspoons chopped thyme

250 ml (9 fl oz/1 cup) olive oil
500 g (1 lb 2 oz) all-purpose potatoes
(such as desiree, kipfler (fingerling)
or pontiac), cut into 5 mm (¼ inch)
rounds

500 g (1 lb 2 oz) eggplants (aubergines),
cut into 5 mm (¼ inch) rounds
500 g (1 lb 2 oz) green capsicums
(peppers), seeded and cut into 3 cm
(1¼ inch) pieces
1 handful flat-leaf (Italian) parsley,
roughly chopped
allioli (page 250), to serve (optional)

Serves 6–8

To make the tomato sauce, score a cross in the base of each tomato and put in a bowl of boiling water for 10 seconds. Plunge into cold water and peel the skin away from the cross. Cut each tomato in half and scoop out the seeds with a teaspoon. Finely chop the tomatoes.

Heat the oil in a heavy-based frying pan and cook the garlic and onion over low heat for 5–6 minutes, or until softened. Increase the heat to medium, add the tomato and thyme and cook for 20 minutes, or until thickened. Season to taste. Preheat the oven to 180°C (350°F/Gas 4).

While the sauce is cooking, heat the oil in a heavy-based frying pan over low heat and cook the potato in batches until tender but not brown. Remove with a slotted spoon or tongs and transfer to a casserole dish measuring about 27 x 21 x 5 cm (10¾ x 8¼ x 2 inches). Season lightly.

Increase the heat to high and cook the eggplant for 3 minutes each side, or until golden, adding a little more oil if necessary. Drain the slices on paper towels, then arrange on top of the potatoes. Season lightly.

Cook the capsicum in the same pan until tender but not browned, adding a little more olive oil if needed. Remove with a slotted spoon, drain on paper towels and arrange on the eggplant. Season lightly. Pour the sauce over the top and bake for 20 minutes. Serve warm, sprinkled with parsley, to accompany fish or meat, or at room temperature with allioli.

queso... The world is discovering Spanish food. And not just the great chefs and dishes, but also the great food products. Even 5 years ago, many would have been hard-pressed to name more than one Spanish cheese: *Manchego.*

The truth is, Spain produces — officially — 100 different types of cheese, 12 of which are covered by a Protected *Denominación de Origen* label. Why officially? Because one market, for instance Cangas de Onis in Asturias, could well have 30 different cheeses for sale.

As already noted, most of these cheeses are made by hand, by cheesemakers who run their own herds of milking animals. Even a famous Spanish cheese like *Cabrales*, from the Picos de Europa in Asturias, is made by small makers in much the same way as it probably was in the time of Pelayo (the legendary 8th century Visigoth and first King of Asturias), with milk from their own herds — often a mixture of cow, goat and sheep. It is matured in mountain caves, where the creamy paste acquires its pungent blue flavour from wild yeasts.

In Extremadura, you will find the cheese that three Michelin star chef Juan Mari Arzak considers the best in Spain: *Torta de la Serena.* Made from raw merino milk, it is a ripe, luscious, oozing, sticky custard-textured centre held (only just) in place by a crusty rind. Scoop it out with a spoon.

One of the finest goat's milk cheeses is the *Queso de Murcia al Vino*, from the province of Murcia on the east coast. During ripening, the rind is washed twice weekly with local wines, either *Tecla* or *Jumilla*, turning the rind red and giving the cheese a floral bouquet and a rich winey flavour.

And of course there is always *Manchego*, the best known of Spain's cheeses, made only from sheep's milk in the provinces of Toledo, Cuenca, Albacete and Ciudad. The best is nutty and sweet with great palate length. From its provincial homes, Manchego travels around Spain, and the world.

Afuega'l Pitu del Aramo, on the other hand, rarely leaves Temia in Asturias. This tart, dense cow's milk cheese whose name, in Asturian dialect, means 'choke the chicken of Aramo', indicating the method for testing the curd. In ancient times a small amount of the curd was given to an unfortunate chicken who choked if it was ready. This is possibly the most ancient cheese produced in Spain but, thankfully, the testing methods have changed somewhat.

500 g (1 lb 2 oz) ripe tomatoes
80 ml (2½ fl oz/⅓ cup) olive oil
400 g (14 oz) potatoes, cut into 2 cm
  (¾ inch) cubes
1 red capsicum (pepper), cut into strips
1 onion, chopped
100 g (3½ oz) jamón or thickly sliced
  prosciutto
150 g (5½ oz) thin green asparagus,
  trimmed

100 g (3½ oz) fresh or frozen green peas
100 g (3½ oz) baby green beans, sliced
2 tablespoons tomato paste (concentrated
  purée)
4 eggs
100 g (3½ oz) chorizo, thinly sliced
2 tablespoons chopped flat-leaf (Italian)
  parsley

Serves 4

Score a cross in the base of each tomato. Put in a bowl of boiling water for 10 seconds, then plunge into cold water and peel away the skin from the cross. Roughly chop the tomatoes.

Heat the oil in a large frying pan and cook the potato over medium heat for 8 minutes, or until golden. Remove with a slotted spoon. Reduce the heat and add the capsicum and onion to the pan. Cut two of the jamón slices into pieces similar in size to the capsicum and add to the pan. Cook for 6 minutes, or until the onion is soft.

Preheat the oven to 180°C (350°F/Gas 4). Reserve four asparagus spears. Add the rest to the pan with the peas, beans, tomato and tomato paste. Stir in 125 ml (4 fl oz/½ cup) of water and season well with salt and ground black pepper. Return the potato to the pan. Cover and cook over low heat for 10 minutes, stirring occasionally.

Grease a large oval ovenproof dish. Transfer the vegetables to the dish, discarding any excess liquid. Using the back of a spoon, make four deep, evenly spaced indentations and break an egg into each. Top with the reserved asparagus and the chorizo. Cut the remaining jamón into large pieces and distribute over the top. Sprinkle with parsley. Bake for about 20 minutes, or until the egg whites are just set. Serve warm.

huevos a la flamenca

pollo relleno

100 g (3½ oz) ham or bacon, chopped
100 g (3½ oz) minced (ground) pork
2 tablespoons chopped flat-leaf
  (Italian) parsley
1 garlic clove, crushed
pinch of ground nutmeg
½ onion, finely diced
1 teaspoon finely chopped oregano
2 tablespoons lemon juice
1 egg, beaten
1.6 kg (3 lb 8 oz) chicken
2 tablespoons vegetable oil

Serves 4

Preheat the oven to 200°C (400°F/Gas 6). To make the stuffing, mix together the ham, pork, parsley, garlic, nutmeg, onion, oregano and lemon juice. Add the beaten egg and mix with your hands until thoroughly combined. Season well.

Wash and pat dry the chicken inside and out, then fill the cavity with the stuffing. Tie the legs together and put the chicken in a roasting tin, coating with the oil. Season with salt and pepper and roast for 30 minutes.

Reduce the heat to 180°C (350°F/Gas 4) and cook for 35–40 minutes, or until the juices run clear when the chicken is pierced between the thigh and body. Allow to rest for 10–15 minutes before carving. Serve a little of the stuffing with each portion of chicken.

250 ml (9 fl oz/1 cup) cream (whipping)
2 garlic cloves, crushed
2 tablespoons chopped flat-leaf (Italian) parsley
1 tablespoon very finely chopped anchovy fillets
600 g (1 lb 5 oz) all-purpose potatoes, peeled
100 g (3½ oz/1 cup) grated Manchego cheese

Serves 4

Preheat the oven to 180°C (350°F/Gas 4). Lightly grease a round 20 cm (8 inch) cake tin.

In a large bowl, combine the cream, garlic, parsley and anchovies, and season well.

Using a sharp knife, cut the potatoes into 5 mm (¼ inch) thin slices (or use a mandolin). Combine the potatoes with the cream mixture, then spread into the cake tin, pressing down with your hands to flatten. Sprinkle the cheese over the top.

Cover with foil and bake for 50 minutes, then remove the foil and bake for a further 15 minutes, or until the top is golden and the potatoes are tender.

spanish-style potato gratin

a little taste of...

The story of Spain's pastries and sweet dishes is rich with tales of conquistadors, Aztecs, Moors and nuns. Chocolate arrived in Spain from Mexico and was embraced immediately; the Moors brought *turrón*, a delicious almond and honey confection, to Europe via Spain, calling it halvo, making it a relative of halva; and the nuns in their convents created such sublime sweets as *tocino de cielo*, literally 'bacon from heaven'.

All around Spain, you will find the most delicious regional pastries—from Santiago de Compostela in Galicia comes *torta de Santiago*; and from Catalonia, *brazos de gitano* (gypsy's arm rolls), a favourite on feast days. But the most celebrated of Spanish dulces is *turrón*, without which no Spaniard could celebrate Easter or Christmas. Weeks before these religious festivals, stores fill up with boxes of *turrón blando* (soft) or the *turrón duro* (hard) *de Alicante* or the soft brown confection called *pan de Cadiz*.

...postres
y dulces

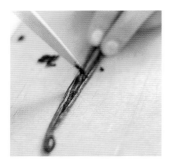

crema catalana

1 litre (35 fl oz/4 cups) milk
1 vanilla bean, split
1 cinnamon stick
zest of 1 small lemon, cut into strips
2 strips orange zest, 4 x 2 cm
  (1½ x ¾ inch)
8 egg yolks
115 g (4 oz/½ cup) caster (superfine)
  sugar
40 g (1½ oz/⅓ cup) cornflour (cornstarch)
45 g (1½ oz/¼ cup) soft brown sugar

Serves 6

Put the milk, scraped vanilla bean, cinnamon stick and lemon and orange zests in a saucepan and bring to the boil. Simmer for 5 minutes, then strain and set aside.

Whisk the egg yolks with the sugar in a bowl for 5 minutes, or until pale and creamy. Add the cornflour and mix well. Slowly add the warm milk mixture to the egg and whisk continuously. Return to the saucepan and cook over low–medium heat, stirring constantly, for 5–10 minutes, or until the mixture is thick and creamy. Do not allow it to boil as it will curdle. Pour into six 185 ml (6 fl oz/¾ cup) ramekins and refrigerate for 6 hours, or overnight.

When ready to serve, sprinkle the top evenly with brown sugar and grill (broil) for 3 minutes, or until it caramelizes.

500 ml (17 fl oz/2 cups) milk
1 cinnamon stick
1 strip lemon zest, 5 x 1 cm (2 x ½ inch)
1 vanilla bean, split
140 g (5 oz) unsalted butter
250 g (9 oz/2 cups) plain (all-purpose)
   flour
145 g (5 oz/²/₃ cup) caster (superfine)
   sugar
4 eggs, separated
125 g (4½ oz/1¼ cups) dry breadcrumbs
vegetable oil, for shallow-frying
1 teaspoon ground cinnamon mixed with
   80 g (2³/₄ oz/¹/₃ cup) caster (superfine)
   sugar, for dusting

Serves 4–6

Grease a 27 x 17 cm (11 x 6½ inch) rectangular tin and line the base and long sides with baking paper. Put the milk, cinnamon stick, lemon zest and scraped vanilla bean in a saucepan and bring to the boil. Turn the heat off.

Melt the butter in a large heavy-based saucepan, then stir in 185 g (6½ oz/ 1½ cups) of the flour. The mixture will form a loose clump around your spoon. Stir over low heat for 30 seconds, then stir in the sugar. Gradually strain the milk into the pan, stirring constantly. Mix for about 10 minutes, or until a smooth mass forms and it leaves the side of the pan. Remove from the heat and stir in the egg yolks one at a time, beating well after each addition (the mixture should now be quite glossy). Spread the custard mixture in the tin, smoothing the surface with your hand. Set aside for 1 hour to cool and set.

Lightly whisk the egg whites together with a fork. Lift the set custard from the tin and carefully cut into 5 cm (2 inch) squares. Dip in the remaining flour to coat all sides. Dip into the egg whites, then the breadcrumbs. Set aside.

Pour the oil in a large frying pan to a depth of 1 cm (½ inch). Heat the oil, add a few squares at a time and cook for about 1 minute per side, or until browned. Drain on paper towels and dust all over with the mixed sugar and cinnamon while still hot. Serve hot or cold.

leche frita

arroz con leche

1 litre (35 fl oz/4 cups) milk
220 g (7¾ oz/1 cup) paella or
    medium-grain rice
1 large strip orange zest
1 cinnamon stick
1 teaspoon natural vanilla extract
145 g (5 oz/²/₃ cup) caster (superfine)
    sugar
orange zest, to garnish (optional)

Serves 6

Put the milk, rice, orange zest, cinnamon, vanilla, sugar and a pinch of
salt in a large saucepan and stir over high heat until the sugar has dissolved.
Allow to just come to the boil, then reduce the heat to a simmer.

Cook the rice mixture over low heat, stirring regularly, for 50 minutes, or
until the rice is tender but not mushy. Stirring not only helps to ensure the rice
mixture does not stick to the bottom of the pan, it also helps to produce a
very creamy texture.

Remove the orange zest and cinnamon stick from the pan with tongs. Serve
the rice pudding warm or cold, garnished with thin strips of orange zest.

4 firm, ripe pears, peeled
80 ml (2½ fl oz/⅓ cup) lemon juice
250 ml (9 fl oz/1 cup) dry red wine
2 cinnamon sticks
220 g (7¾ oz/1 cup) sugar
8 slices lemon

Serves 4

Rub the pears with the lemon juice. Put the red wine, cinnamon sticks, sugar, lemon slices and 250 ml (9 fl oz/1 cup) of water in a saucepan over low heat and simmer gently until the sugar dissolves. Bring to the boil, then reduce the heat and simmer for about 15 minutes. Add the pears and simmer for a further 20 minutes, carefully turning occasionally to ensure even colouring. Leave the pears to soak in the syrup overnight, if possible.

Remove the pears and simmer the syrup over high heat for about 15 minutes, or until it thickens slightly.

Serve the pears whole, drizzled with the syrup.

pears cooked in red wine

flan de naranja

275 g (9¾ oz) caster (superfine) sugar
200 ml (7 fl oz) fresh orange juice,
**   strained**
7 egg yolks, at room temperature
1 egg

Serves 4

Preheat the oven to 170°C (325°F/Gas 3). Lightly grease four 125 ml
(4 fl oz/½ cup) ramekins or moulds with oil spray and place in a baking dish.

Put 80 g (2¾ oz/⅓ cup) of the sugar and 60 ml (2 fl oz/¼ cup) of water
in a small saucepan and stir gently over low heat until the sugar dissolves.
Increase the heat to a low boil and cook for about 10 minutes, or until the
mixture becomes golden and smells like caramel. Quickly divide the toffee
among the moulds and tilt to cover the bases.

Put the orange juice and remaining sugar in a small saucepan over low
heat and stir gently until the sugar dissolves. Increase the heat, bring to
the boil and cook for 2 minutes, or until the mixture is slightly syrupy. Leave
to cool for 10 minutes.

Put the egg yolks and whole egg in a bowl and beat with a wooden spoon.
Pour the cooled orange juice onto the eggs, stirring until well combined.
Pass the mixture through a sieve, then spoon into the moulds.

Pour enough boiling water into the baking dish to come halfway up the side
of the ramekins. Bake for 15 minutes, then carefully remove the ramekins from
the water and cool to room temperature. Chill completely in the refrigerator
(this will take about 2 hours).

When ready to serve, dip the moulds in hot water for 10 seconds, then invert
onto serving plates.

4 thick slices of day-old bread
150–200 ml (5–7 fl oz) sweet sherry
 or Malaga wine
60 ml (2 fl oz/¼ cup) vegetable oil
2 eggs, beaten with a dash of milk
1 teaspoon ground cinnamon mixed with
 2 tablespoons caster (superfine) sugar,
 for dusting
honey, to serve (optional)

Serves 4

Dip both sides of the bread slices in the sherry, then drizzle on any leftover liquid. Leave to sit for a few minutes to absorb the sherry.

Heat the oil in a frying pan over medium heat. Dip the bread slices in the beaten egg, then fry on each side for 3–4 minutes, or until golden brown.

Drain on paper towels, then dust with the combined cinnamon and sugar and drizzle with honey.

torrijas

la pastelería... The contents of a Spanish sweet shop are ruled by region and season. Come Easter and Christmas, for example, they will be filled with *turrón*, the soft version from Jijona, north of Alicante, and the crunchy *turrón* from Alicante itself. Although some say that *turrón*, made from honey and almonds, dates from pre-Roman times, it's clear to most food historians that it came with the Moors.

As did many of the sweets of Catalonia, such as the *bisbalenc* of the coastal Ampurdan region (a sort of strudel filled with sweet summer squash paste and topped with pine nuts and sugar) and *panellets* (marzipan balls coated with grilled (broiled) pine nuts). Very un-Moorish is the most famous dessert of the region, now on menus all around Spain: *flan catalan* or *crema catalana*. Unlike its French cousin (*crème brûlée*), it is made with the addition of lemon juice and cinnamon.

Every region of Spain has its own sweets or pastries. Try leaving Majorca without eating an *ensaimada* (a spiral-shaped pastry made with lard and dusted with sugar, often eaten at breakfast). Then there are *filloas* (lace pancakes from Galicia); the rich and luscious *mamía* (a milk-based pudding made with ewe's milk in the Basque countries and the Catalan Pyrenees); or *recuit* (the Catalan version of ricotta, a dessert cheese eaten with honey and walnuts).

But it is the nuns in the convents of Spain, especially in Andalusia, Extremadura and Castile, who are the keepers of the ancient and traditional sweet recipes. For hundreds of years, these recipes, based on the simplest of ingredients—eggs, sugar, flour, lard or oil, sesame seeds and cinnamon—were closely guarded secrets, handed down from generation to generation as unchanged as the articles of faith. Many convents have their own specialities. For example, in Osuna, the Dominican Santa Catalina convent makes *capiruletas* (a heavy uncooked custard cream made with egg yolks, sugar, ground almonds and cinnamon). There are various convents where you will find those desserts called *yemas*, based on candied egg yolks, the most famous of which (*yemas de San Leandro*) were—and still are—made by the nuns of San Leandro in Seville.

Finally it should be noted that the Spanish don't tend to cook sweets in their homes, nor do traditional Spanish restaurants serve a great variety of sweets. At the end of a meal, you are more likely to be offered seasonal fruit, cheese or a product from the local *pastelería*. Those who insist on dessert when dining out will have to make do with the ever-present *flan catalan*.

almond turrón ice cream

115 g (4 oz/½ cup) caster (superfine)
  sugar
50 g (1¾ oz/⅓ cup) whole blanched
  almonds, roasted
6 egg yolks
80 g (2¾ oz/⅓ cup) caster (superfine)
  sugar, extra
100 ml (3½ fl oz) sweet sherry
435 ml (15¼ fl oz/1¾ cups) cream
  (whipping)

Serves 6

To make the almond praline, combine the sugar and 60 ml (2 fl oz/¼ cup) of water in a saucepan. Stir over low heat with a metal spoon until the sugar has dissolved. Increase the heat, bring to the boil and cook for 6 minutes, or until the mixture is dark golden brown (but not burnt).

Scatter the almonds onto a greased baking tray, then pour on the toffee and set aside to harden.

Mix the egg yolks and sugar in a bowl with an electric beater until pale and creamy. Whisk in the sherry. Transfer the custard to a heatproof bowl over a saucepan of simmering water, making sure the bowl does not touch the water. Whisk constantly for 10–15 minutes, or until the custard is thick and foamy. Remove from the heat at this point, cover and leave to cool.

Whip the cream until firm, but not stiff. When the custard is cool, gently fold in the cream using a large metal spoon or spatula until combined. Pour the mixture into a shallow metal container—a cake tin with a capacity of at least 1 litre (35 fl oz/4 cups) is ideal. Chill in the freezer until frozen around the edges. Remove and beat with an electric beater until smooth. Pour the custard back into the container and re-freeze. Repeat this process three times, or until the ice cream is soft and not icy.

Crush the praline and fold it through the ice cream after the final mixing.

For the final freezing, put the ice cream in an airtight container and cover with a piece of greaseproof paper and a lid. Freeze for at least 3 hours,

175 g (6 oz/¹⁄₂ cup) honey
125 ml (4 fl oz/¹⁄₂ cup) sweet dark sherry
  (such as Pedro Ximenez)
¹⁄₄ teaspoon ground cinnamon
18 large dried figs
18 whole blanched almonds
100 g (3¹⁄₂ oz) dark chocolate, cut
  into shards
thick (double/heavy) cream, for serving
  (optional)

Serves 6

Combine the honey, sherry, cinnamon and figs with 375 ml (13 fl oz/
1¹⁄₂ cups) of water in a large saucepan over high heat. Bring to the boil, then
reduce the heat and simmer for 10 minutes. Remove the pan from the heat
and set aside for 3 hours. Remove the figs with a slotted spoon, reserving
the liquid.

Preheat the oven to 180°C (350°F/Gas 4). Return the pan of liquid to the
stove and boil over high heat for 5 minutes, or until syrupy, then set aside.
Snip the stems from the figs with scissors, then cut a slit in the top of each
fig with a small sharp knife. Push an almond and a few shards of chocolate
into each slit. Put the figs in a lightly buttered ovenproof dish and bake for
15 minutes, or until the chocolate has melted.

Serve three figs per person, with a little of the syrup and a dollop of cream.

higos rellenos

torta de santiago

**450 g (1 lb) whole blanched almonds,
   lightly roasted**
150 g (5½ oz) unsalted butter, softened
400 g (14 oz) caster (superfine) sugar
6 eggs
150 g (5½ oz) plain (all-purpose) flour
2 teaspoons grated lemon zest
2 tablespoons lemon juice
icing (confectioners') sugar, for dusting

Serves 8

Preheat the oven to 170°C (325°F/Gas 3). Lightly grease a 24 cm (9½ inch) spring-form cake tin. Finely grind the almonds in a food processor.

Using electric beaters, cream the butter and sugar in a bowl until light and fluffy. Add the eggs one at a time, beating well after each addition. Using a large metal spoon, fold in the flour, ground almonds and the lemon zest. Stir until just combined and almost smooth.

Pour the batter into the prepared tin and bake for 1 hour 20 minutes, or until a skewer inserted in the centre comes out clean. Cool for 5 minutes, then brush the top with lemon juice. Transfer to a wire rack and cool completely. Dust with icing sugar in a cross pattern, using a stencil if you wish.

375 g (13 oz/3 cups) plain (all-purpose)
   flour
125 ml (4 fl oz/½ cup) olive oil
125 ml (4 fl oz/½ cup) beer
60 ml (2 fl oz/¼ cup) anisette liqueur
115 g (4 oz/½ cup) caster (superfine)
   sugar
40 g (1½ oz/¼ cup) sesame seeds
2 tablespoons aniseeds

Makes 16

Preheat the oven to 200°C (400°F/Gas 6). Lightly grease a baking tray and line with baking paper.

Sift the flour and 1 teaspoon of salt into a large bowl and make a well. Add the oil, beer and anisette and mix with a large metal spoon until the dough comes together. Transfer to a lightly floured surface and knead for about 4 minutes, or until smooth. Divide the dough in half, then divide each half into eight portions.

In a small bowl, combine the sugar, sesame seeds and aniseeds.

Make a small pile of the seed mixture on a work surface and roll out each portion of dough over the mixture to a 15 cm (6 inch) round, embedding the seeds underneath. Put the rounds on a baking tray with the seeds on top and cook for 5–6 minutes, or until the bases are crisp. Put the biscuits 10 cm (4 inches) under a hot grill (broiler) for about 40 seconds, or until the sugar caramelizes and the surface is golden. Transfer to a wire rack to cool.

aniseed biscuits

gypsy's arm cake

200 g (7 oz) dark chocolate, broken into pieces
80 ml (2½ fl oz/⅓ cup) strong black coffee
7 eggs, at room temperature, separated
150 g (5½ oz) caster (superfine) sugar
1 tablespoon icing (confectioners') sugar mixed with 2 tablespoons unsweetened cocoa powder
1 teaspoon rich sweet sherry or rum
300 ml (10½ fl oz) cream (whipping), whipped

Serves 8–10

Preheat the oven to 180°C (350°F/Gas 4). Grease a 29 x 24 x 3 cm (11½ x 9½ x 1¼ inch) Swiss roll tin (jelly roll tin) and line with baking paper.

Melt the chocolate with the coffee in a bowl over a small saucepan of simmering water, stirring occasionally, until almost melted. Remove from the heat and stir until smooth. Set aside to cool a little.

Beat the egg yolks and sugar in a large bowl until light and creamy, then stir in the chocolate mixture. Whisk the egg whites in a separate bowl until soft peaks form. Using a large metal spoon or rubber spatula, gently fold the whites into the chocolate mixture. Pour into the lined tin and bake on the middle shelf of the oven for 15 minutes, or until the cake springs back when lightly touched in the middle. Turn off the oven and open the door slightly.

After 10 minutes, turn out the cake onto a clean tea towel (dish towel) that has been dusted with the sugar and cocoa mixture. Leave for 30 minutes, or until cool.

Sprinkle the top of the sponge with the sherry and spread with the whipped cream. Roll the cake up, using the tea towel to help you but removing it as you go. Wrap in plastic wrap and refrigerate until ready to slice and serve.

285 g (10 oz/1¼ cups) caster (superfine)
  sugar
1 vanilla bean, split
1 egg
6 egg yolks

Makes about 36 pieces

Preheat the oven to 180°C (350°F/Gas 4). Put 120 g (4¼ oz/½ cup) of the sugar and 2 tablespoons of water in a small saucepan over low–medium heat. Stir with a metal spoon until all the sugar has dissolved. Bring to the boil and cook for a further 10–15 minutes, or until the toffee is a rich golden colour. Remove from the heat and, taking care not to burn yourself, pour into a 20 cm (8 inch) square cake tin, tilting to cover the base.

Meanwhile, put 250 ml (9 fl oz/1 cup) of water in a saucepan with the vanilla bean and remaining sugar. Bring to the boil, then reduce the heat and simmer for 10 minutes, or until the liquid has reduced to a slightly syrupy consistency. Leave to cool a little. Remove the vanilla bean.

Using electric beaters, beat the whole egg and egg yolks until smooth. Slowly add a stream of the cooled sugar mixture while beating on high. Once combined, strain the liquid onto the toffee mixture in the cake tin.

Put the cake tin in a larger baking dish. Pour enough boiling water into the larger dish to come one-third of the way up the side of the cake tin. Bake for 30 minutes, or until just set. Cool completely.

When ready to serve, dip the tin into a hot water bath for 30 seconds to loosen the caramel. Run a knife around the custard and unmould onto a serving plate. Drizzle any remaining caramel over the top and cut into small squares to serve.

tocino de cielo

bizcocho

6 eggs, at room temperature
380 g (1²/₃ cups/13 oz) caster
  (superfine) sugar
2 teaspoons grated lemon zest
185 g (6½ oz/1½ cups) plain
  (all-purpose) flour, sifted

Serves 8

Preheat the oven to 160°C (315°F/Gas 2–3). Lightly grease and line a 24 cm (9½ inch) spring-form tin. Using electric beaters, beat the eggs and sugar for 15 minutes, or until light and creamy. Beat in the lemon zest. Using a large metal spoon or spatula, gently fold the flour into the egg mixture.

Pour the batter in the prepared tin and bake for 1 hour 10 minutes. Turn off the oven and leave the oven door open for 5 minutes, then remove the cake from the oven and leave to cool completely in the tin.

chocolate and churros...

Of all the foods the Spanish brought back from the New World (potatoes, tomatoes, capsicums (peppers) and chillies) none was more quickly and enthusiastically embraced than chocolate.

There was a simple reason for this. The Aztecs of Mexico told the soldiers of Hernán Cortés' army that chocolate was an aphrodisiac. Moctezuma, the Aztec king, employed 20 women solely to prepare his drinking chocolate, often ceremonially served in leopard-skin cups. The Spanish soldiers observed that chocolate harvest time was accompanied by wild orgies.

But the chocolate drunk by the Aztecs was very different from the drink enjoyed at today's *churrerias* (chocolate and *churros* shops). The Aztecs spiked their chocolate drink with spices, ground flowers and chilli, and coloured it with achiote, a seed that dyed the drink red.

As you would expect, this dangerous drink was not welcomed by the clergy. Even when the aphrodisiac rumour was finally put to bed, there was argument over whether the drinking of chocolate broke the Lenten fast.

Curious, then, that some time later, the bitter drink of the Aztecs was transformed by the nuns at a convent in Guajaca into the delicious concoction enjoyed today, simply by adding sugar. Later, it was accepted by and, indeed, embraced by the clergy—so much so that it became the favoured breakfast of the Grand Inquisitor, prepared for him by the nuns in his service—an ironic reminder of Moctezuma's chocolate maidens.

Walk into a *churreria* on any given morning and you will find carousers on their way home and workers starting the day sitting side by side, dunking their *churros* in chocolate so thick the *churros* stand up in it. This *espeso* (thick) chocolate is achieved by the addition of cornflour (cornstarch).

And what is a *churro*? One of the *frutas del sartén*, a fruit of the frying pan. A light flour and water batter is forced through a ridged pipe — which gives the *churro* its distinctive form — and then piped into boiling hot oil, before being cut into edible lengths.

This combination of chocolate and *churros* is, to the traditional Spaniard, not complete without a small glass of aniseed liqueur. It is perhaps the most Spanish way to start the day — or end the night.

110 g (3¾ oz/½ cup) sugar
1 teaspoon ground cinnamon
30 g (1 oz) butter
150 g (5½ oz) plain (all-purpose) flour
½ teaspoon finely grated orange zest
¼ teaspoon caster (superfine) sugar
2 eggs
oil, for deep-frying

HOT CHOCOLATE
2 tablespoons cornflour (cornstarch)
1 litre (35 fl oz/4 cups) milk, plus
   2 tablespoons, extra
200 g (7 oz) good-quality dark chocolate,
   chopped
sugar, to taste

Serves 4

Combine the sugar and cinnamon and spread the mixture out on a plate.

Put the butter, flour, orange zest, caster sugar, 170 ml (5½ fl oz/⅔ cup) of water and a pinch of salt in a heavy-based saucepan. Stir over low heat until the butter softens and forms a dough with the other ingredients. Continue to cook for 2–3 minutes, stirring constantly, until the dough forms a ball around the spoon and leaves a coating on the base of the pan.

Transfer the dough to a food processor and, with the motor running, add the eggs. Do not overprocess. If the dough is too soft to snip with scissors, return it to the pan and cook, stirring, over low heat until it is firmer. Spoon the dough into a piping bag fitted with a 5 mm (¼ inch) star nozzle.

Heat the oil in a wide saucepan to 180°C (350°F), or until a cube of bread browns in 15 seconds. Pipe lengths of batter 6–8 cm (2½–3¼ inches) long into the oil, a few at a time. An easy technique is to pipe with one hand and cut the batter off using kitchen scissors in the other hand. Cook the churros for about 3 minutes, or until puffed and golden, turning once or twice. Drain each batch on paper towels. While still hot, toss them in the sugar mixture and serve at once.

To make the hot chocolate, mix the cornflour and 2 tablespoons of milk to a smooth paste. Put the chocolate and remaining milk in a saucepan and whisk constantly over low heat until just warm. Stir 2 tablespoons of chocolate milk into the cornflour paste, then return all the paste to the milk. Whisking constantly, cook the mixture until it just begins to boil. Remove from the heat, add sugar to taste, and whisk for another minute. Serve with the hot churros.

churros and hot chocolate

polvorones

250 g (9 oz/2 cups) plain (all-purpose)
   flour, sifted
½ teaspoon ground aniseed
125 g (4½ oz/1 cup) icing (confectioners')
   sugar, sifted
250 g (9 oz) softened butter
1 egg yolk
1 teaspoon lemon juice
2 teaspoons dry sherry

Makes 20

In a large bowl combine the flour, aniseed, 1 tablespoon of icing sugar and a pinch of salt.

Beat the butter with electric beaters until pale and creamy, then beat in the egg yolk, lemon juice and sherry until well combined. Beat in half the flour mixture with the electric beaters, then stir in the remaining flour with a wooden spoon. Gather the dough into a ball with your hands, cover with plastic wrap and refrigerate for 1 hour. Preheat the oven to 150°C (300°F/Gas 2).

Roll out the dough on a floured surface to a 1 cm (½ inch) thickness. Using a 5 cm (2 inch) cutter, cut into cookies. Bake on an ungreased baking tray for 20 minutes, or until the cookies are light brown and firm. Allow to cool slightly, then roll the cookies in the remaining icing sugar. Cool completely, then roll in the icing sugar again. Store the cookies, covered with any remaining icing sugar, for up to 2 weeks in an airtight container.

1 bizcocho, baked in a square or
   rectangular tin (page 241)
115 g (4 oz/½ cup) caster (superfine)
   sugar
125 ml (4 fl oz/½ cup) sherry or Malaga
   wine
ground cinnamon, for dusting
whipped cream (whipping), to serve

Serves 8–10

Cut the cooled bizcocho into squares.

Put the sugar and 125 ml (4 fl oz/½ cup) of water in a small saucepan over low heat and stir with a metal spoon until the sugar has dissolved. Bring to the boil for 4 minutes. Add the sherry and boil for 3 minutes, or until syrupy.

Drizzle the syrup evenly over the cake squares. Dust the tops with cinnamon and serve with whipped cream.

drunken cakes

basics

ALLIOLI

2 egg yolks
4 garlic cloves, crushed
60 ml (2 fl oz/¼ cup) white wine vinegar or lemon juice
125 ml (4 fl oz/½ cup) vegetable oil
125 ml (4 fl oz/½ cup) olive oil

Makes about 250 ml (9 fl oz/1 cup)

Put the egg yolks and garlic in a food processor with 1 tablespoon of the vinegar or lemon juice. While the motor is running, add the oils in a very slow stream until you have a thick mayonnaise. If at some point the mayonnaise becomes too thick, add the remaining vinegar and continue adding the rest of the oil. Season well.

Allioli will keep in an airtight container in the refrigerator for 4–5 days.

PEELED TOMATOES

Score a cross in the base of each tomato with a knife. Put the tomatoes in a bowl of boiling water for 10 seconds, then plunge into a bowl of cold water. Remove from the water and peel the skin away from the cross—it should slip off easily. Remove the seeds with a teaspoon if desired, and chop the flesh.

SANGRIA

1½ tablespoons caster (superfine) sugar
1 tablespoon lemon juice
1 tablespoon fresh orange juice
750 ml (26 fl oz) bottle of red wine
   (preferably Spanish)
500 ml (17 fl oz/2 cups) lemonade
2 tablespoons gin
2 tablespoons vodka
1 lemon
1 orange
1 lime
ice cubes, to fill pitcher

Serves 10

Put the caster sugar, lemon juice and orange juice in a large pitcher or bowl and stir until the sugar has dissolved. Add the red wine, lemonade, gin and vodka.

Cut the lemon, orange and lime into halves, remove the seeds and slice all the fruit thinly. Add the slices to the pitcher and fill with ice. Stir well.

ROASTED RED CAPSICUMS

Cut each capsicum (pepper) into four flattish pieces and carefully remove the seeds and membrane. Arrange the pieces in a single layer on a baking tray and cook under a hot grill (broiler) until the skins are blackened and blistered.

Put the peppers in a large bowl and cover with plastic wrap (or put them in a plastic bag) and leave to cool for 10 minutes.

Peel away the skins and cut the flesh into thin strips.

glossary

Aniseed (also known as anise or anise seed) These greenish brown, licorice-flavoured seeds are used in both sweet and savoury cooking and also to make *anis*, an alcoholic beverage similar to schnapps. Buy the seeds whole as once ground they lose flavour.

Bacalao The Spanish term for cod which has been salted and dried. It must be soaked for about 20 hours before use to rehydrate the fish and to remove the excess salt. Once prepared, it flakes easily and is popular in fritters, but is also cut into larger pieces for poaching, simmering or baking in various sauces.

Bay leaves Glossy green leaves sold fresh or dried and used to add a strong, slightly peppery flavour to wet savoury dishes and occasionally to puddings and custards. The fresh leaves are a little stronger than the dried.

Besan (chickpea flour) A high-protein flour made by finely grinding chickpeas. Chickpea flour has a nutty flavour and is ideal for making batter for deep-fried foods and for thickening sauces.

Calasparra rice (also known as paella rice) A medium-grained, high-quality absorbent white rice grown in the Calasparra region that is traditionally used to make paella. *Bomba* is one variety of *Calasparra* rice and can sometimes be found labelled as such.

Caperberries The fruit of the caper bush, which appear after the flowers. They are usually preserved in brine and are often served as an accompaniment or garnish (much like olives).

Capers The small flowers of the caper bush, which are preserved in brine and sometimes just salt. They should be rinsed well before use. They have a piquant flavour and are used in small amounts in dressings, salads and as a garnish. The smaller the caper, the more aromatic and therefore expensive.

Cava A quality Spanish sparkling white wine made by the same bottle fermentation method as Champagne. Cava is refreshing to drink, and is also used to make sweet and savoury sauces.

Cayenne (also known as cayenne pepper) A powder made from ground red chilli peppers native to South America. It is very pungent and spicy and should be used sparingly. It is often added to wet dishes for heat and is sometimes sprinkled over cheese-topped dishes before baking or grilling (broiling) as the flavours are complementary.

Chickpeas Small legumes commonly used in rustic, home-style cooking. Pale brown or yellow in colour, they are commonly available dried and need to be soaked and cooked before being consumed; however, you can now find them already prepared and tinned for convenience. Once soaked, or after the initial boiling, chickpeas should be rubbed between your hands and rinsed to help remove their skins.

Chillies Available fresh, dried or roasted, chillies belong to the capsicum (pepper) family and are native to South and Central America, from where they were taken by the Spanish and Portuguese into the Mediterranean. There are many different varieties of chilli and they vary dramatically in size, heat and flavour. The seeds and inner membranes should be removed if less heat is desired.

Chorizo The best known of all Spanish sausages, chorizo is made from minced (ground) or chopped pork and pork fat, flavoured with sweet and hot paprika (pimentón), garlic and black pepper. Sometimes sold soft for cooking in wet dishes (such as soups or stews), it is more commonly found as a hard, cured sausage that can be eaten as is, but is often sliced and fried, then eaten as a snack or added to wet dishes.

Cumin (sometimes known as cummin) Indigenous to the East Mediterranean, the seeds are used whole or ground to flavour savoury dishes and breads. The pungent, slightly nutty flavour is enhanced by dry-roasting before use.

Jamón Spanish ham, resembling good-quality prosciutto, is available in different grades and varies in flavour and texture, depending on its region of origin. *Jamón Iberico* is ham from the black Iberian pigs, which are fed mainly on acorns, figs and sometimes olives, giving the meat great flavour and aroma. The ham is salted, air-dried then matured for about 2 years. *Jamón serrano*, or mountain ham, is from the fattened white pigs of the Sierra Nevada region, which are salted then air-cured for at least a year. Jamón is extremely flavoursome and tender and is often added to cooked dishes or simply eaten on its own.

Manchego cheese One of Spain's most famous cheeses, originally made from the milk of Manchego sheep from the La Mancha region. A semi-firm cheese with a rich but mellow flavour which alters with age. Sold as fresh, semi-cured and cured—the texture firming and flavour deepening at each of these stages. It is perfect for everyday eating and has wonderful melting properties.

Morcilla A northern Spanish sausage made from pig's blood, similar to black pudding. It is very rich and often spiced with cinnamon, cloves and nutmeg. Some variations include rice, potato, garlic, white beans, onion or fennel. They are boiled before being hung up to dry and are then sometimes smoked. Often added to stews or casseroles or sautéed and crumbled into stuffings and dishes such as scrambled eggs.

Navy beans (also known as haricot beans or pea beans) One of the many members of the haricot bean family, navy beans are small white legumes sold dried, and are perfect for soups and stews as they require long, slow cooking. If not available, other members of the haricot bean family can be substituted (for example, cannellini, pinto or borlotti (cranberry) beans).

Paprika (pimentón) Small red capsicums (peppers) varying in heat from mild to hot are dried, sometimes smoked, then ground for use in savoury dishes both for flavour and colour. The rusty red powder is most commonly sold as sweet or mild (*dulce*), medium hot (*agridulce*) and hot (*picante*). Smoked paprika is also popular in certain regions of Spain and a small amount adds a distinctive smoky flavour to savoury foods.

Pimiento/Pimientos del piquillo Pimiento are a type of red capsicum (pepper). *Pimientos del piquillo* are small, hot, red capsicums, which are preserved in oil in a tin or jar after being roasted and charred, then carefully peeled. Ready for use, the whole *pimiento del piquillo* can be stuffed then deep-fried or baked in sauce, or chopped and added to salads or other dishes. Pimiento can also be puréed to form the basis of a sauce or soup. Small amounts of the red pimiento are often used to stuff green olives.

Saffron The orange-red stigma of one species of the crocus plant is the most expensive spice in the world due to the fact that one flower contains only three stigmas, which are laboriously hand picked and then dried. Fortunately, only a little is needed when cooking. Sold in both thread and powdered form, beware of cheap imitations. Saffron is best toasted, then soaked in warm liquid for a few minutes before use—this helps to bring out the flavour and colour.

Squid ink (also known as cuttlefish ink) Used to colour and flavour Spanish rice dishes and sauces for seafood. The black ink is stored in a sac that can be removed from whole squid and cuttlefish but is also available in sachets from fishmongers or good delicatessens. It has a subtle savoury flavour that is not at all fishy, as one might expect.

Tocino Spanish fat bacon which is salted and air-cured but not smoked. Often sold covered with a layer of crystalline salt. It is used in stews and soups and, when made from Iberian pigs, is much sought after.

Vine leaves (grape leaves) Large green leaves of the grape vine are used in Mediterannean and Middle Eastern cookery, mainly to wrap foods before grilling (broiling), roasting or simmering. Commonly available in brine in jars, tins or packets, they are also sometimes sold fresh (these should be blanched in hot water until pliable before use). Vine leaves in brine should be rinsed or briefly soaked in cold water to remove the salty brine.

index

First published in 2006 by Murdoch Books Pty Limited.
This edition published 2010

Murdoch Books Australia
Pier 8/9, 23 Hickson Road, Millers Point NSW 2000
Phone: 61 (0) 2 8220 2000
Fax: 61 (0) 2 8220 2558
www.murdochbooks.com.au

Murdoch Books UK Limited
Erico House, 6th Floor, 93-99 Upper Richmond Road,
Putney, London SW15 2TG
Phone: + 44 (0) 20 8785 5995
Fax: + 44 (0) 20 8785 5985
www.murdochbooks.co.uk

Chief Executive: Juliet Rogers
Publishing Director: Kay Scarlett

Publisher: Lynn Lewis
Senior Designer: Heather Menzies
Designer: Alex Frampton
Cover Designer: Erika Cvejic
Photographer: Alan Benson (location and recipes)
Additional Photography: Ian Hofstetter (recipes)
Production: Kita George

National Library of Australia Cataloguing-in-Publication Data
Title: A little taste of Spain
ISBN 978 1 74196 962 7 (pbk.)
Notes: Includes index.
Subjects: Cookery, Spanish
Dewey Number: 641.5946

PRINTED IN CHINA

IMPORTANT: Those who might be at risk from the effects of salmonella food poisoning (the elderly, pregnant women, young children and those suffering from immune deficiency diseases) should consult their GP with any concerns about eating raw eggs.

CONVERSION GUIDE: You may find cooking times vary depending on the oven you are using. For fan-forced ovens, as a general rule, set the oven temperature to 20°C (35°F) lower than indicated in the recipe. We have used 20 ml (4 teaspoon) tablespoon measures. If you are using a 15 ml (3 teaspoon) tablespoon, for most recipes the difference will not be noticeable. However, for recipes using baking powder, gelatine, bicarbonate of soda (baking soda), small amounts of flour and cornflour (cornstarch), add an extra teaspoon for each tablespoon specified.